Oracle WebLogic Server 11gR1 PS2: Administration Essentials

Install, configure, deploy, and administer Java EE applications with Oracle WebLogic Server

Michel Schildmeijer

BIRMINGHAM - MUMBAI

Oracle WebLogic Server 11gR1 PS2: Administration Essentials

First published: September 2011

Production Reference: 2150911

Published by Packt Publishing Ltd.
Livery Place
35 Livery Street
Birmingham B3 2PB, UK.

ISBN 978-1-849683-02-9

www.packtpub.com

Cover Image by Tony Shi (shihe99@hotmail.com)

Credits

Author
Michel Schildmeijer

Reviewers
Vivek Acharya
Izaak de Hullu
Balamurali Kothandaraman
Wickes Potgieter

Acquisition Editor
Rukshana Khambatta

Development Editor
Rukshana Khambatta

Technical Editors
Arun Nadar
Jenecia Menezes

Copy Editor
Laxmi Subramanian

Project Coordinator
Zainab Bagasrawala

Proofreader
Denise Dresner

Indexer
Monica Ajmera Mehta

Graphics
Valentina D'Silva
Nilesh R. Mohite

Production Coordinators
Aparna Bhagat
Prachali Bhiwandkar

Cover Work
Aparna Bhagat

About the Author

Michel Schildmeijer was born in the Netherlands, in 1966. He has lived his whole life in the capital, Amsterdam. After mid-school, he started studying pharmacy. After four years, he had to fulfill his military service, in the Royal Dutch Air Force, working in a pharmacy.

After this, he got a job as a quality inspector for a pharmacy company, but after about two years he switched his job for a position in a hospital's pharmacy, where he worked for over 10 years.

In the meantime he got married, and he and his wife Tamara had two boys, Marciano and Robin. He went through a difficult period in his personal life, when his wife got extremely ill for some time and he had to take all the responsibility for managing his family. Fortunately, he got intensive support from his parents-in-law, who helped greatly with taking care of his kids.

Within his pharmacy job, around 1994, he became acquainted with the Medical Information System which was being used to structure patients' medical history and information. This was a system running on HP UNIX, a MUMPS SQL database and text-based terminal. He started learning UNIX and MUMPS to give operational support. By then he became enthusiastic, so he switched jobs and started working for some IT companies. Around 2000 he started using Oracle on a big banking application for settlements and clearance. The system was running on Oracle 7, AIX UNIX, BEA WebLogic, and BEA Tuxedo. This was the first time he worked with WebLogic. From then he became more and more specialized in middleware and Oracle. He worked on many projects. Around 2006 he started working on several projects for IBM, in the Oracle Middleware team, administering, configuring, and tweaking large Oracle Middleware systems with Oracle SOA Suite, Oracle Portal, Oracle HTTP, and many more.

In 2008, he worked for Randstad Holding, and got more and more specialized in developing the middleware infrastructure around applications. He started an investigation into migrating the Oracle Application Server 10g and SOA Suite 10g to the 11g platform. Around that period Oracle acquired BEA.

From working in Brussels for Belgacom, a big Telco company, he started his current job as Oracle Fusion Middleware Architect, for AMIS, an IT company specialized in Oracle and JAVA.

His focus was always on developing the infrastructure for many companies, and advising them how to migrate or build a new middleware platform based on the latest 11g techniques. He also became an instructor, teaching all the basics of Oracle WebLogic 11g, just as in this book, but from a practical point of view.

The reason for his writing this book is because he thinks that middleware infrastructure and administration have become an important part in the application landscape, even though the focus in a migration project of an application is always on application logic and functionality, and less on the pre-conditions of how this application will be distributed to end-clients or other systems.

I would like to thank my wife Tamara, whose life is a difficult struggle sometimes

Janny and Steef, who took care of my kids

Marciano and Robin, my great kids

All the reviewers, including Izaak, my colleague from AMIS

And all those who supported me in an unusual way

About the Reviewers

Vivek Acharya is an Oracle Consultant working as a professional freelancer. He has been a developer, consultant, and architect for approximately seven years. He is an Oracle Certified Expert as an Oracle Fusion-SOA 11g Implementation Specialist.

He has experience and expertise in Oracle Fusion – SOA, BPM, BAM, Mediator, B2B, BI, AIA, WebLogic, Oracle E-Business Suite – PLM, SCM, Finance, Logistics, and Retail.

He loves all things that have to do with Oracle Fusion Applications, Oracle SOA, Oracle BPM, Cloud Computing, Salesforce, ODI, OSB, SaaS, and BSM.

He is the author of a couple of books and enjoys playing the synthesizer and cricket.

You can find him at `http://www.linkedin.com/pub/vivek-acharya/15/377/26a` or write him at `vivek.oraclesoa@gmail.com` or read him at `http://acharyavivek.blog.co.in`.

Izaak de Hullu is a senior architect with Amis Services in Nieuwegein, the Netherlands. He has worked on enterprise integration projects with Java, Oracle Fusion Middleware, BEA Aqualogic, and Cordys for the last eight years. In those years, he has gained experience with the WebLogic Application Server versions 8 and up. Before that he worked as a knowledge engineer designing and building knowledge-based systems for a large Dutch government organization. He holds a Masters Degree in Computer Science, specializing in Information and Knowledge Engineering, at the University of Twente [NL]. He lives in Amstelveen with his wife and three daughters. In his free time he likes to read about modern history, to cook with friends, and to play guitar.

Balamurali Kothandaraman (Bala) has more than 15 years of experience in IT architecture, including full blueprint of reference and enterprise architecture. He is currently working as a director of Enterprise Architecture with Standard and Poor's (S&P), a division of the McGraw-Hill Companies, leading efforts to design, develop, and implement technology-enabled business information solutions encompassing multiple specializations, platforms, and technologies. Prior to S&P he worked for more than nine years with Oracle | BEA Systems Inc. as a Principal Technologist and for many consulting houses such as 3i Infotech, Technosoft, and HCL Technologies, where he designed, developed, and implemented enterprise solutions for various customers.

Bala is a globally recognized speaker and workshop modulator on various major events like JavaOne, BEAWorld conferences, and BEA Support Webinars & WebLogic User Groups. Bala recently reviewed the Packt Publishing book *EJB 3.0 Database Persistence with Oracle Fusion Middleware 11g* and constantly blogs about WebLogic Server at `http://weblogicserver.blogspot.com`.

> Thanks to my wife Subathra and children, Magathi and Amritha, for their understanding and patience which helped me through this whole process and to achieve many other things in my life.

Wickes Potgieter has been working as a product specialist for over 10 years. His main focus was on the BEA WebLogic suite of products and after the Oracle acquisition of BEA Systems, focused on the Oracle Fusion Middleware suite of products. His experience ranges from architecture and infrastructure design, administration, development, pre-sales, training-to-performance tuning of the Oracle Fusion Middleware products, JVM, and custom applications.

He and his colleague formed a specialized consulting company in 2003 with offices in the United Kingdom and South Africa, covering customers in the EMEA region. They are Oracle Gold partners and have 30 technical consultants specializing on the Oracle Red Stack of products. Their branch in the UK is called TSI-Systems Limited (`www.tsisystems.co.uk`) and in South Africa is called EAI Specialized Services (`www.eai.co.za`).

> I would like to thank my wife Mary Jane for her patience and assisting me through all the late nights. Thank you to all my friends and family for constant encouragement.

www.PacktPub.com

Support files, eBooks, discount offers and more

You might want to visit www.PacktPub.com for support files and downloads related to your book.

Did you know that Packt offers eBook versions of every book published, with PDF and ePub files available? You can upgrade to the eBook version at www.PacktPub.com and as a print book customer you are entitled to a discount on the eBook copy. Get in touch with us at service@packtpub.com for more details.

At www.PacktPub.com, you can also read a collection of free technical articles, sign up for a range of free newsletters and receive exclusive discounts and offers on Packt books and eBooks.

http://PacktLib.PacktPub.com

Do you need instant solutions to your IT questions? PacktLib is Packt's online digital book library. Here, you can access, read and search across Packt's entire library of books.

Why Subscribe?

- Fully searchable across every book published by Packt
- Copy and paste, print and bookmark content
- On demand and accessible via web browser

Free Access for Packt account holders

If you have an account with Packt at www.PacktPub.com, you can use this to access PacktLib today and view nine entirely free books. Simply use your login credentials for immediate access.

Instant Updates on New Packt Books

Get notified! Find out when new books are published by following @PacktEnterprise on Twitter, or the *Packt Enterprise* Facebook page.

Table of Contents

Preface

Oracle's WebLogic 11g Server is an application server for building and deploying enterprise Java EE applications. WebLogic's infrastructure supports the deployment of many types of distributed applications and is an ideal foundation for building applications based on a Service Oriented Architecture. This book will guide you through the important administration aspects of WebLogic Server.

This book will teach administrators the techniques for installing and configuring Oracle WebLogic Server and how to deploy Java EE applications using the Administration Console, command-line interface, and scripting tools such as WLST. This book starts with a good overview of the needed techniques in the middleware world of today. Clear explanations of definitions and concepts of JEE and how Oracle WebLogic fits into that are also provided. The book then dives into performing routine Oracle WebLogic Server administration functions, and how to deploy different types of Java EE applications to WebLogic Server.

What this book covers

Chapter 1, Oracle WebLogic: Your First Step into a Middleware World! will give you an overview of Oracle WebLogic Architecture, WebLogic Domain concept, WebLogic Managed Servers, different tier architectures, and software architecture of the Oracle WebLogic Server.

Chapter 2, The Beginning: Planning and Installation focuses on installing the WebLogic software. This chapter will teach you the various aspects of the Oracle WebLogic software. Also the reader will learn the different default locations where the software has been placed.

Chapter 3, Oracle WebLogic Software Installed; What's Next? covers the planning strategy and configuration of a domain, the different options to choose, and different modes such as graphical- and console-based. By the end of the chapter we will understand what a domain is and how to create a basic domain, we will know the different templates, and what to configure during domain creation.

Chapter 4, Getting in Control: Operation Basics will guide you through the different tools an administrator can use to manage the WebLogic Server Domain, such as starting/stopping, use of the Administration Console, and command line tools.

Chapter 5, Managed Servers and the Node Manager; here you will learn the basic terms and techniques of Managed Server Instances and the Node Manager. You will learn how to create and configure your Managed Server Instance, and also how to set up a proper Node Manager configuration.

Chapter 6, Deploy your Applications in Oracle WebLogic; here you will learn the very basics of deployment, how WebLogic handles deployments, which tools an administrator can use for deployment, and some strategies about how to approach the deployment process.

Chapter 7, Connecting to the Outside World: JDBC and JMS will teach you how to set up your WebLogic Domain using additional resources when communicating with databases (JDBC) or Messaging Systems (JMS).

Chapter 8, Making your WebLogic Mission-Critical: Clustering; you will learn how in this 24/7 economy, systems have to be highly available and performing at the top of their capabilities. In this chapter, you will also learn all about clustering best practices.

Chapter 9, The Heart of Oracle WebLogic Server: The JVM will explain the Java Virtual Machine, an important component in the WebLogic Domain, along with some best practices about how to gain an optimal configuration for your WebLogic Domain.

Chapter 10, What if Something Goes Wrong? will give you a start in the areas you could begin to troubleshoot. Although there are many possible scenarios, in real life often the same issues will appear and can be easily tackled.

Chapter 11, Configuring and Analyzing Logging, will help you to determine the possible failures, which is an important administrator's task, and it will also help you to make a start to configure it to your needs.

Chapter 12, Keeping your WebLogic Secure: Security and Protection is where you will encounter the many aspects of being secure in your software environment.

Chapter 13, WLST: Makes an Administrator's Life Easier; here you will become familiar with the strong capabilities of the WLST, customizing WLST, and custom MBeans features.

What you need for this book

A Linux environment (such as Oracle Enterprise Linux) and the Oracle WebLogic installer package which can be downloaded from Oracle Technet.

Who this book is for

If you are a middleware administrator looking for a quick guide for performing routine and important WebLogic Server administration functions, including configuring WebLogic Server and deploying Java EE applications, then this is the perfect book for you. It could be helpful if you already have some experience as an Oracle or JAVA developer, or as an OS, Web server, or middleware administrator. Also database administrators who want to learn more about Oracle WebLogic can use this book for guidance.

Conventions

In this book, you will find a number of styles of text that distinguish between different kinds of information. Here are some examples of these styles, and an explanation of their meaning.

Code words in text are shown as follows: "JVMs trigger `java.lang.OutOfMemoryError` when there is insufficient memory to perform some task".

A block of code is set as follows:

```
connect("username","password")
edit()
startEdit()
cmo.setConsoleEnabled(true)
save()
```

Any command-line input or output is written as follows:

```
unpack-template=path_of_jar_file-domain=path_of_domain_to_be_created
[-user_name=username] [-password=password] [-app_dir=application_
directory] [-java_home=java_home_directory] [-server_start_mode=dev|prod]
[-log=log_file] [-log_priority=log_priority]
```

New terms and **important words** are shown in bold. Words that you see on the screen, in menus or dialog boxes for example, appear in the text like this: "The **SSL** tab for the specified Server Instance is used to configure the **BEA Hostname Verifier**".

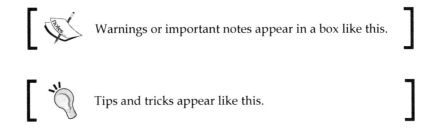

> Warnings or important notes appear in a box like this.

> Tips and tricks appear like this.

Reader feedback

Feedback from our readers is always welcome. Let us know what you think about this book—what you liked or may have disliked. Reader feedback is important for us to develop titles that you really get the most out of.

To send us general feedback, simply send an e-mail to feedback@packtpub.com, and mention the book title via the subject of your message.

If there is a book that you need and would like to see us publish, please send us a note in the **SUGGEST A TITLE** form on www.packtpub.com or e-mail suggest@packtpub.com.

If there is a topic that you have expertise in and you are interested in either writing or contributing to a book, see our author guide on www.packtpub.com/authors.

Customer support

Now that you are the proud owner of a Packt book, we have a number of things to help you to get the most from your purchase.

Downloading the example code

You can download the example code files for all Packt books you have purchased from your account at `http://www.PacktPub.com`. If you purchased this book elsewhere, you can visit `http://www.PacktPub.com/support` and register to have the files e-mailed directly to you.

Errata

Although we have taken every care to ensure the accuracy of our content, mistakes do happen. If you find a mistake in one of our books—maybe a mistake in the text or the code—we would be grateful if you would report this to us. By doing so, you can save other readers from frustration and help us improve subsequent versions of this book. If you find any errata, please report them by visiting `http://www.packtpub.com/support`, selecting your book, clicking on the **errata submission form** link, and entering the details of your errata. Once your errata are verified, your submission will be accepted and the errata will be uploaded on our website, or added to any list of existing errata, under the Errata section of that title. Any existing errata can be viewed by selecting your title from `http://www.packtpub.com/support`.

Piracy

Piracy of copyright material on the Internet is an ongoing problem across all media. At Packt, we take the protection of our copyright and licenses very seriously. If you come across any illegal copies of our works, in any form, on the Internet, please provide us with the location address or website name immediately so that we can pursue a remedy.

Please contact us at `copyright@packtpub.com` with a link to the suspected pirated material.

We appreciate your help in protecting our authors, and our ability to bring you valuable content.

Questions

You can contact us at `questions@packtpub.com` if you are having a problem with any aspect of the book, and we will do our best to address it.

1
Oracle WebLogic: Your First Step into the Middleware World!

Ever wondered how information about the different areas, such as personal, financial, medical, or whatever you can think of, is processed, distributed, and secured in a safe way? The digital, electronic, and complex world today needs good and solid solutions to make sure that they fulfill the needs of our entire society.

You as an IT technician can play an important role in that world. You will have to translate business needs into technical solutions. And business needs are very demanding these days. Computer systems need to be available 24/7 and must deliver a solid environment where no loss of data is allowed.

And in our fast economy, systems need to perform at the top of their abilities, because applications running on them are highly critical and information needs to be delivered in a limited amount of time.

IT technicians play an important role in building a solid solution for all these requirements. In this book, you will discover Oracle's very solid solution, presented as the Oracle WebLogic Server.

The very first steps into middleware

Nowadays, middleware is the key component in IT infrastructure. It connects various systems to each other, lets users interact with their applications, and lets them manipulate data. That's why big software vendors, such as Oracle, have a so-called strategic platform for their middleware. Let's take a deeper look into the unveiled secrets of the middleware world!

Middleware is computer software that connects software components, people, and their applications.

The software consists of a set of services that allows multiple processes running on one or more machines to interact. This technology evolved to provide for interoperability in support of the move towards coherent distributed architectures, which are most often used to support and simplify complex distributed applications.

Middleware, as the name suggests, sits "in the middle" of the application software that may be working on different operating systems. It is similar to the middle layer of three-tier single system architecture, except that it is stretched across multiple systems or applications. Examples include EAI software, telecommunications software, transaction monitors, and messaging-and-queuing software.

The pre-middleware era

Before the introduction of middleware platforms, applications had isolated programs running on isolated computers. As an administrator, if a new version of the program came out, you had to go by every client computer to update or reinstall the software.

Also, when problems occurred, it was very hard to determine what the cause was, because all resources ran locally on the client machine, each with their own settings and configurations. Later on, things got more evolved by pushing software from a central store to the client PCs, but still they ran isolated, and was very difficult to administer.

With the upcoming Internet during the 90's, applications also began to evolve from client computers into centralized environments, accessed through a web browser, such as Internet Explorer. The birth of middleware environments was a fact, and more and more different vendors began to develop their own strategic platforms.

What is a middleware environment?

There is no strict definition of a middleware environment, but in general one can say: middleware is software that connects components, systems, users, and their applications. It includes web servers, application servers, and other tools that provide application development, deployment, execution, and delivery. Middleware is able to handle all kinds of information technology based on XML, SOAP, web services, and SOA.

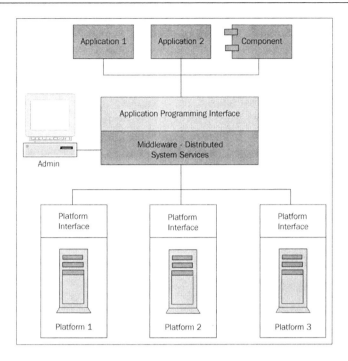

An Application Server plays the key role in a middleware environment. In fact, this is the platform that connects all systems with each other, with the many plugins, resources, and other interfaces that the Application Server delivers.

The Java EE Application Server

Oracle WebLogic implements the JEE standards. JEE is the standard for JAVA Server programming and runtime JAVA.

JEE has a wide variety of APIs (Application Programming Interface) in it, such as JDBC, RMI, e-mail, JMS, web services, XML, and more. These components are also part of the WebLogic Server environment and will be discussed in the coming chapters. JEE also features some specifications for components that are unique to Java EE. Besides leveraging the APIs, JEE also contains Enterprise JavaBeans, connectors, servlets, portlets, Java Server pages, and several web service technologies. This allows developers to create enterprise applications that integrate with legacy technologies.

A Java EE application server can handle transactions, security, scalability, concurrency, and management of the components that are deployed to it, in order to enable developers to concentrate more on the business logic of the components rather than on infrastructure and integration tasks.

The case: Your company needs middleware!

In this book we will be an employee of a fictive company, where you act as a senior technical consultant. You have a very demanding boss who is a very stressed person, because he receives a lot of pressure from his boss about the status of several projects. But you, middleware expert that you are, can provide him with all the solutions that are discussed in this book, and in the end, your boss (and you of course) is very happy. So go for the "Hollywood happy ending" when you finish this book.

FinanceFiction Enterprises

You work for a big worldwide financial company with many customers around the world. The following are some of the key aspects of your company:

- Company size: 60,000 employees worldwide
- Estimated equity: $250 billion
- Yearly profit: $25 billion (but under pressure because of bad performing systems!)
- Key customers: Large companies, such as oil industries, telco's worldwide
- Key departments:
    ◦ Marketing and communication
    ◦ Financial and accounting services
    ◦ Customer relations
    ◦ Settlements, clearance and security
    ◦ Human resources

Your company is an international financial institution serving many end-customers all over the world including large enterprises that trust your company for all their financial transactions. So it's obvious that a good computer infrastructure is needed to deliver the highest level of service to the customers. Also, internally your company depends on good infrastructure. The current infrastructure needs a thorough renewal because most of the technologies are outdated. A lot of legacy systems have become more and more isolated. Customers begin to complain that they experience have all kinds of problems; your boss gets more and more pressured and nervous. But you, being the cool and calm technician that you are, provide him with the solution:

The Oracle Fusion Middleware Solution

Oracle WebLogic is part of the Oracle Fusion Middleware Solution as Oracle has called its middleware product stack.

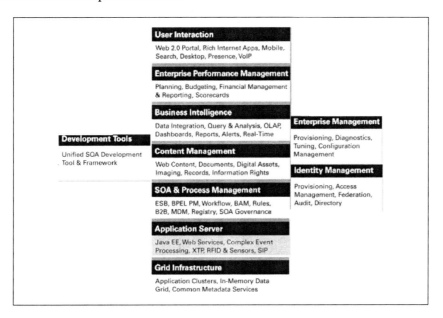

The previous diagram gives a schematic overview of the entire stack of the Oracle middleware portfolio. Of course, in this book we will focus mainly on Oracle WebLogic, but we will occasionally touch on some other areas as well.

Oracle WebLogic is the key platform in the entire Fusion Middleware stack. All kinds of different layers of software have the Oracle WebLogic Server as the base platform.

From OC4J to WebLogic

With the introduction of the "i" after its main releases (8i, 9i), Oracle began to put more and more focus on Internet and browser-based computing. Oracle builds from version 9i its own J2EE server, based on HTTP (Apache) and Oracle Containers for Java (OC4J). Each OC4J was a Java Virtual Machine. On top of OC4J, many applications could be deployed such as Oracle Forms & Reports, Oracle Portal, Oracle Discoverer Web version (all on version 10.1.2), and Oracle SOA Suite (BPEL, ESB and OWSM) on 10.1.3.

The following diagram shows the OC4J versus WebLogic comparison:

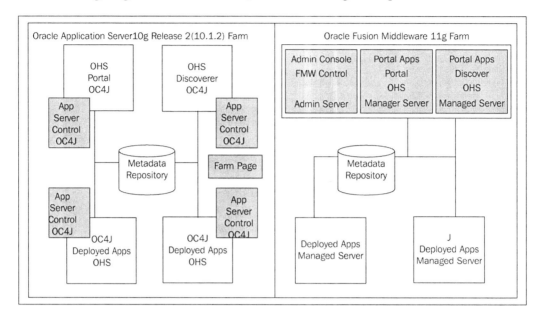

In July 2008, Oracle launched its new 11g Middleware platform: Oracle WebLogic 11g.

However, with the acquisition of Sun and BEA, a lot of customers were added as well. So it will take some time to get all customers in line!

Oracle WebLogic architecture and terminology

Finally! Your big day is here. Your company, FinanceFiction has decided to modernize its outdated middleware solutions with the Oracle Fusion Middleware stack.

Your boss keeps smiling all day, because your department has been chosen to be the pilot and do a proof of concept. You've been asked to do some preliminary research in order to explain to the non-technical board members what the Oracle WebLogic Server can do for FinanceFiction.

Oracle WebLogic: A JEE Server

Oracle WebLogic is, as said earlier, the middleware infrastructure environment that all kinds of applications—Oracle or non-Oracle—make use of. Oracle WebLogic is a **JEE (Java Enterprise Edition) Server.** More about the JEE concept will be discussed later in this chapter.

Oracle WebLogic technology facts

You have been promoted by your boss to do the research about Oracle WebLogic. A catchy one-liner you could use in your presentation is:

Oracle WebLogic Server is a scalable, enterprise-ready, Java Platform Enterprise Edition (Java EE) application server.

The WebLogic Server infrastructure supports the deployment of many types of distributed applications and is an ideal foundation for building applications based on Service Oriented Architectures (SOA). SOA is a design methodology aimed at maximizing the reuse of application services.

Although this sounds like a line of a typical salesperson, it's still true. The WebLogic Server delivers implementation of the Java EE 5.0 specification, and provides a standard set of APIs for creating distributed Java applications that can access a wide variety of services, such as databases, messaging services, and connections to external enterprise systems.

This is exactly what your company needs: more interaction between the diversity of your systems.

WebLogic Server enables enterprises to deploy mission-critical applications in a robust, secure, highly available, and scalable environment.

Another one, but also true. WebLogic is easy to scale and can be set up with continuity for the business so that they wouldn't notice if a system is down.

Next, we will dive a little deeper into the basic concepts of the WebLogic Server.

The WebLogic domain structure

The basic administrative unit for a WebLogic Server is called a domain. A domain is a logically related group of WebLogic Server resources that you manage as a unit. A domain always includes the minimum of one instance called the Administration Server. The Administration Server is a central point of contact for server instances and system administration tools. A domain may also include additional WebLogic Server instances called Managed Servers and clusters.

A Managed Server might be part of a WebLogic Server cluster. A cluster is a group of WebLogic Server instances that work together to provide scalability and high-availability for applications. A Managed Server in a cluster can act as a backup for services such as JMS that are hosted on another server instance in the cluster. Applications are normally deployed in a Managed Server.

The domain can run in two modes:

- Development mode: A domain running in development mode does not require a password during startup of the Administration Server. You also can do autodeploy of your applications, as some other parameters are not that strictly configured.

- Production mode: Running in production mode needs passwords, encryption of files at a higher level, and some parameters within the resources (such as JDBC, JMS) are strictly configured.

You can have multiple domains based on:

- Physical location

- Logical division of applications (backend application domain, frontend application domain)

- Size (smaller manageable units instead of one huge domain)

The next diagram shows the flow of the several steps creating a domain. This will be discussed later on.

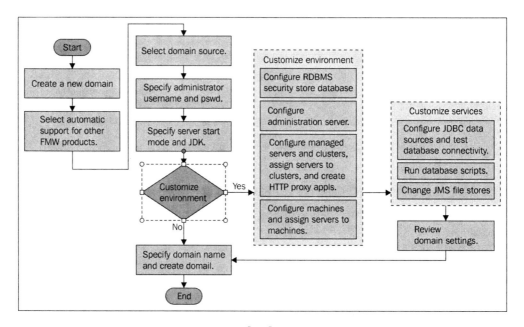

Administration Server

Each WebLogic domain has an Administration Server. As its name suggests, it's the base administration unit to handle all kinds of administration tasks within the WebLogic domain. An Administration Server does all its tasks within the Java Virtual Machine (JVM). The Administration Server can be accessed through a web browser. You can deploy your application on an Administration Server but it is recommended to create Managed servers and deploy your application in a Managed server and leave the Administration Server for configuration and maintenance purposes only. There will allways be only one Administration Server per domain.

Managed Servers

Other instances running in their own JVM than the Administration Server that are within a WebLogic domain are called Managed Servers. As stated, it runs in its own JVM. A Managed server can start independently from an AdminServer, if configured so.

Two or more Managed servers can be configured as a WebLogic Server cluster to increase scalability and availability. In a WebLogic Server cluster, most resources and services are deployed identically on each Managed Server, enabling failover and load balancing. A single domain can contain multiple WebLogic Server clusters, but can also contain nonclustered Managed Servers.

The main difference between clustered and nonclustered Managed Servers is the support for failover and load balancing handled by the WebLogic domain (one can configure clustering outside WebLogic of course). These features are available only in a cluster of Managed Servers.

Managed Servers are used to facilitate applications and their resources, as described in the next section.

Resources

"I don't have enough resources available!", you hear your boss scream on the phone to the program manager, who is demanding quicker results in order to get the project going. Your boss is running out of his office yelling, "Work harder, faster, more!!".

You get a slight smile on your lips. Through your research, you already began to understand that the WebLogic Server is very efficient in managing its resources. Your boss could learn managing his own resources as the WebLogic Server does.

Both a WebLogic Administration Server and a Managed Server manage their resources and services efficiently to such an extent that nothing is wasted.

The domain delivers resources and services required by Managed Servers and hosted applications deployed in the domain. The domain configuration includes information about the environment.

The domain configuration also includes information about resources and services associated with applications hosted on the domain. Examples of these resources and services include:

- Application components, such as EJBs or JSPs
- Security providers
- Resource adapters
- JDBC data sources
- JMS servers or other messaging resources
- Store-and-forward service
- Persistent store
- Startup classes
- Diagnostics and monitoring services

Resources and services can be limited to one or more Managed Servers in the domain, rather than being available to the domain as a whole. You can deploy resources and services to selected Managed Servers or to a cluster.

A deeper look into Managed Servers will be handled in *Chapter 5, What is a Managed Server?*.

Oracle WebLogic—a JEE server… but what is JEE?

Oracle WebLogic is a JEE application server, that is Java Enterprise Edition. But what does this mean?

The JEE distributed system

A WebLogic infrastructure containing multiple managed JEE application servers is called a distributed system.

It divides the work among several independent modules. The failure of a single module has less impact on the overall system, which makes the system more:

- Available
- Scalable
- Maintainable

JEE standards allow:

- Modularization of complex hardware and software
- A larger portion of the project costs to go toward solving business software needs

Java EE is a widely used platform for server programming in the Java programming language. The Java EE platform differs from the standard edition of Java, in that it adds libraries which provide functionality to deploy fault-tolerant, distributed, multi-tier Java software, based largely on modular components running on one or more JEE application servers.

Applications deployed with Java EE technologies are standardized, have specification guidelines, are written in Java, and are deployable to any JEE application server.

The following diagram shows an example of a typical JEE architecture:

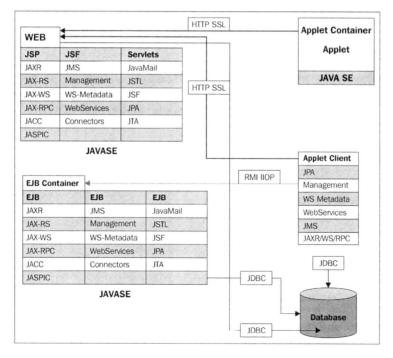

In this overview, you can see practically all components that are a part of the JEE. We will discuss some of them in this chapter.

JEE Resources

As your boss was screaming for resources, well, you can present him the JEE distributed system. It contains a lot of resources, such as:

- Java Servlets
- Java Server Pages (JSP)
- Enterprise JavaBeans (EJB)
- Java Database Connectivity (JDBC)
- Java Naming and Directory Interface (JNDI)
- Java Transaction API (JTA)
- Java Message Service (JMS)
- Java Authentication and Authorization (JAAS)
- Java Management Extensions (JMX)
- Java EE Connector Architecture (JCA)

We will look into the different components and how they interact with each other to get an overview of how a (WebLogic) JEE system works.

Java Servlets

A **servlet** is a Java program that executes on the server, accepts client requests, and generates dynamic responses. An example of a servlet is an HttpServlet that accepts HTTP requests and generates other HTTP Servlets, which may be packaged in a **WAR** file as a Web application.

Simple code of an HttpServlet:

```
import java.io.IOException;
import java.io.PrintWriter;
import javax.servlet.ServletException;
import javax.servlet.http.HttpServlet;
import javax.servlet.http.HttpServletRequest;
import javax.servlet.http.HttpServletResponse;
public class HelloWorld extends HttpServlet {
  public void doGet(HttpServletRequest request, HttpServletResponse
response)
      throws ServletException, IOException {
```

```
PrintWriter out = response.getWriter();
out.println("<!DOCTYPE HTML PUBLIC \"-//W3C//DTD HTML 4.0 " +
            "Transitional//EN\">\n" +
            "<html>\n" +
            "<head><title>Hello WWW</title></head>\n" +
            "<body>\n" +
            "<h1>Hello WWW</h1>\n" +
            "</body></html>");
    }
}
```

Downloading the example code

You can download the example code files for all Packt books you have purchased from your account at http://www.PacktPub.com. If you purchased this book elsewhere, you can visit http://www.PacktPub.com/support and register to have the files e-mailed directly to you.

Java Server Pages (JSP)

A JavaServer page is a way to generate dynamic HTML and XML. This is done by Java code and some predefined actions, called JSP actions.

JSPs use a JSP compiler to access the Java code and loads this into a servlet, as you can see in the following code:

The following is an example snippet of a JSP generated servlet:

```
package jsp_servlet;
 import java.util.*;
 import java.io.*;
 import javax.servlet.*;
 import javax.servlet.http.*;
 import javax.servlet.jsp.*;
 import javax.servlet.jsp.tagext.*;
 import example ; // Imported as a result of <%@ page
 import="com.foo.bar" %>
 import …
class _myservlet implements javax.servlet.Servlet, javax.servlet.jsp.
HttpJspPage {
    // Inserted as a
    // result of <%! int serverInstanceVariable = 1;%>
    int serverInstanceVariable = 1;

    …
```

```
    public void _jspService( javax.servlet.http.HttpServletRequest
request,
    javax.servlet.http.HttpServletResponse response )
    throws javax.servlet.ServletException,
    java.io.IOException
    {
        javax.servlet.ServletConfig config = …; // Get the servlet
config
        Object page = this;
        PageContext pageContext = …;              // Get the page
context for this request
        javax.servlet.jsp.JspWriter out = pageContext.getOut();
        HttpSession session = request.getSession( true );
        try {
            out.print( "<html>\r\n" );
            out.print( "<head>\r\n" );
```

Java Naming and Directory Interface (JNDI)

The API used for accessing resources is JNDI. It's a layer built for accessing naming and directory services (naming service such as an internet address). It uses a directory kind of structure to bind the objects and is accessible by passing simple strings showing logical directory structure such as "jdbc/DB1" (a JNDI for a JDBC service).

A developer does not need to code resource references by using the computer, host, or database names, he /she can use the JNDI name. This makes the code much more generic and can be easily reused. Therefore it's independent of the underlying structure. In the following diagram you can see how a web service connects to an EJB using JNDI.

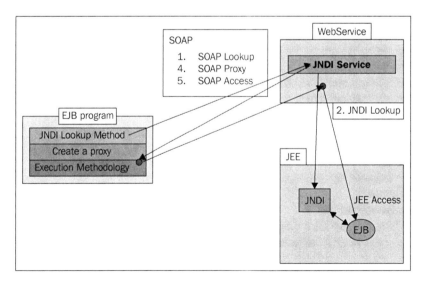

Enterprise JavaBeans (EJB)

The Enterprise Java Bean is a JAVA API server-side component that handles business logic of an application. The beans are running in an EJB Container on a JEE Server.

Many Oracle products, such as the Oracle SOA Suite, use EJBs. As an administrator, it's good to know the basic knowledge of EJB and how they behave in a WebLogic environment. As an example, it can help you to know how to size your JVMs.

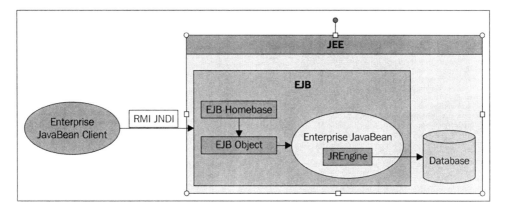

From the previous diagram, you can see that the EJB client (can be an application) connects over RMI (Remote Method Invocation) by using JNDI naming.

Java Database Connectivity (JDBC)

An important resource in your Oracle WebLogic is most certainly your set of JDBC resources. Java Database Connectivity (JDBC) is also a standard Java API that consists of a set of classes and interfaces.

Developers use JDBC to write database applications and execute SQL statements. JDBC requires the use of a driver; implements database-specific connectivity, and statement handling. WebLogic provides many drivers for different kinds of databases. It's used internally for metadata purposes and for application and business purposes.

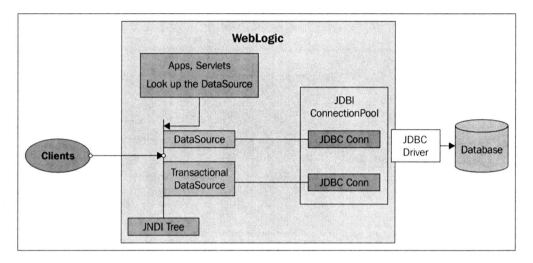

As noted, JDBC can be used for supporting the infrastructure (for example, the Oracle SOA Suite Infra application) or for customer-related data.

Java Transaction API (JTA)

JTA is an API too that allows distributed transactions, such as XA transactions. It contains three elements: a high-level application transaction demarcation interface, a high-level transaction manager interface intended for an application server, and a standard Java mapping of the X/Open XA protocol intended for a transactional resource manager. It supports user transaction in EJB, JNDI, and Servlets. The WebLogic Server can process the transaction process that is addressed by the JTA. Application servers handle the bulk of application operations and take some of the load off the end-user application.

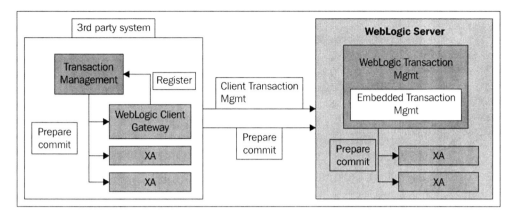

Java Message Service (JMS)

Java Message Service is an API for accessing message-oriented middleware.

The interface supports:

- Point-to-point communication
- Publish/subscribe ("pub/sub") communication
- Guaranteed message delivery
- Transactional participation
- Application- or system-scoped resources
- Interoperability with other messaging systems

JMS is a way of loosely coupled messaging. It uses a queuing mechanism; the publisher puts a message on the queue without knowing that it will be picked up. The subscriber then picks up the message. It knows that the message is for that person because it's embedded in the message header.

Key components of JMS are:

- JMS provider
    - ° The JMS interface for a Message Orientated Middleware (MOM)
- JMS client
    - ° Produces and/or receives messages
- JMS producer/publisher
    - ° Creates and sends messages

- JMS consumer/subscriber
  - ◦ Receives messages

- JMS message
  - ◦ The actual message

- JMS queue
  - ◦ An area that contains messages that have been sent and are waiting to be read

- JMS topic
  - ◦ A distribution mechanism for publishing messages

The next diagram shows the WebLogic JMS Server Architecture:

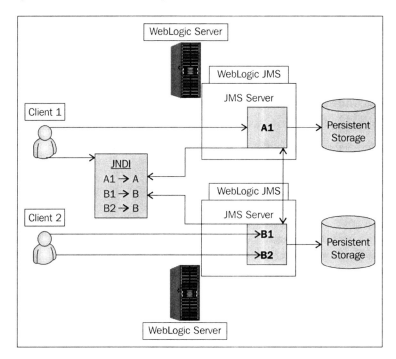

Java Authentication and Authorization Service (JAAS)

Java Authentication and Authorization Service (JAAS) is a Java-based security management framework. It supports Single Sign-On, and is implemented within the WebLogic Server. Terms that are used in the WebLogic JAAS implementation are security providers and realms.

A realm is a collection of users and groups that are controlled by the same authentication policy. Security providers implement the underlying security framework for your JEE applications. The default security providers can be used or one can implement his/her own security provider within the WebLogic Server. The following diagram shows an example of an authentication process:

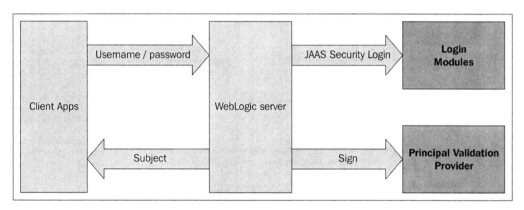

JMX

Java Management Extensions is a technology that lets you implement management interfaces for Java applications. The specification describes MBeans, which are the building blocks of JMX. One can access these MBeans (Managed Beans) using the WebLogic Scripting Tool (WLST). It supports managing and monitoring for all kinds of services.

JMX is an open technology that is not specific to WebLogic, but is a part of JEE/JSR specification.

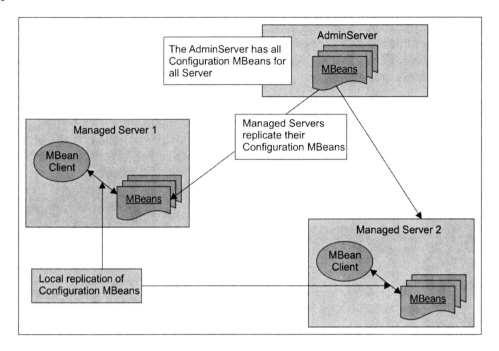

Java EE Connector Architecture (JCA)

Another connector API is called the JCA adapter. It connects EIS (Enterprise Information System) with the so-called resource adapters, deployed in an archive (RAR).

For instance, you could use a SAP resource adapter to connect to a SAP EAI.

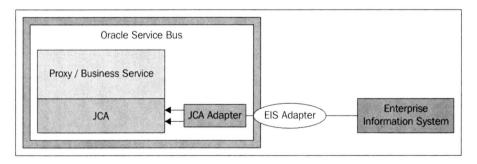

With JCA, one could connect to many Enterprise systems, such as SAP, PeopleSoft, and Siebel, among others.

Secondary components in the JEE architecture

Besides the components that are directly managed in a JEE system, there are also external, yet influential, components that should be discussed briefly here.

HTTP clients and servers

During the 90's, with the expanding Internet, the web server began to play a key role. A web server — as the name suggests — provides web content, mainly with the HTTP(S) protocol, and sometimes also through FTP and others. It can handle some scripting such as JavaScript and CGI.

A HTTP client connects to a web server, and depending on the role of the web server, passes the request through to an application server. Web clients can connect through JAVA, web browsers, FTP, and Mail.

Proxy servers

A proxy server is more like an intermediate between clients and web servers or application servers. It can speed up connections by caching frequently requested pages. It can apply policies and mask the identities of the clients. Sometimes it is also referred to as a gateway.

Firewalls

Firewalls are a well-known and always topical issue. Firewalls can block unauthorized users from outside a company, detect intrusions, and scan for malware and spyware. In fact, they are the lock on the door to the outside world.

Key players in the middleware market

During your research into whether Oracle's WebLogic is the best option for FinanceFiction, you came across some other middleware vendors and their products. Although it was not your assignment to investigate them, you thought it was wise to have a quick look at the kind of solutions other companies provided.

IBM WebSphere

IBM provides a wide variety of middleware products, with its strategic platform called WebSphere Application Server. In general, it provides the same resources as Oracle WebLogic does.

Some of the products are:

- WebSphere Application Server
- WebSphere Business Integration Toolset
- WebSphere InterChange Server
- WebSphere MQ
- WebSphere Message Broker
- WebSphere Adapters
- WebSphere Process Server
- WebSphere Portal Server

TIBCO

Another vendor is TIBCO, which is also a provider of infrastructure software for companies. Some of its products are:

- TIBCO ActiveMatrix
- TIBCO BusinessEvents
- TIBCO Collaborative Information Manager
- TIBCO Silver
- TIBCO Spotfire

SAP

SAP is a software vendor that provides Enterprise Software (as discussed in the JCA adapter). It specializes in ERP (Enterprise Resource Planning) software, and provides a lot of business solutions such as supply chain management and data management. Technical platforms are NetWeaver and some specialized frameworks.

Open source-like Apache Software Foundation

The open source community also provides middleware solutions. One of the well-known solutions is Apache, that is also used within Oracle Fusion Middleware.

Apache is an open source web server for all kinds of operating systems such as AIX, Solaris, Windows, and AS 400.

The first version came out in 1995 as an answer to the Netscape web server, but unlike Netscape, Apache still exists and is still popular. It's being used by a lot of vendors as their HTTP server.

In the Oracle Webtier Utilities, Apache is used as the web server (Oracle HTTP Server). To integrate the Webtier, a new module is used, which is `mod_ohs`.

The big day: Presenting your research!

How can you best present your research? Here you go:

Presentation to the board

Your boss has asked you to do the big presentation for the members of the board. He's very nervous and agitated, because getting this assignment would give his (and your) department a big boost in the company. Also, the introduction of new technologies would give your department a big lift in your company.

So, you think about what you need to tell them without sounding like a salesperson selling a product, in this case, Oracle WebLogic.

In general, you could ask yourself, "Why Oracle WebLogic anyway? And why not some other player in the market?"

Decisions to make

Of course you could recommend another platform, but that was not your assignment. Because your company already uses a lot of other Oracle products, the main goal should be to introduce Oracle WebLogic as the middleware platform.

As with any other platform, technology, or solution there are always pros and cons to choose or not to choose a certain direction. But during your research, you became convinced that "Oracle WebLogic 11g is the future!!"

Your presentation...

The first slide of your presentation could be the following one:

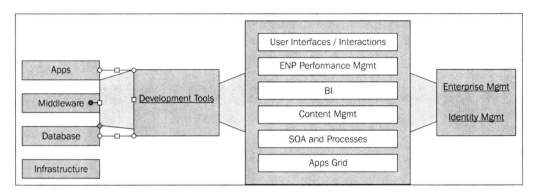

You need to tell your audience about Oracle WebLogic being a middleware platform, which is needed as a key component in the many different environments in the company. Also, you have to explain to them how to reduce costs by introducing SOA and process management, also on the WebLogic platform, and about the platform's scalability, stability, and performance.

Driven by your enthusiasm, you see the members changing their expressions into smiling ones, and your boss, who is sitting behind them, is giving you the thumbs-up. It looks like all your research and effort will be rewarded.

But there's one grumpy old man, who always has negative opinions, including about this whole subject; he (although he has zero technical knowledge) tries to bombard you with all kinds of questions that could prove that his negative view is right.

For example, he asks you: "We have a lot of different legacy systems, and it will cost a whole lot of money to hire all the developers to recode to the WebLogic platform," and he triumphantly laughs at his colleagues. You even see your boss's eyelid tremble, but when you tell him about the many integration solutions, such as the JCA adapter, even he becomes enthusiastic.

Then, after a two-hour session, you finish your presentation, and your boss gives you a big compliment. The final decision will be taken later.

Summary

This chapter contained your first careful steps into the middleware world. Although a middleware environment can become very complex, many companies underestimate the administration and configuration aspect of it. As big projects mainly focus on developing new applications and functionality, they often forget to think about the infrastructure, or do so just at a very late stage of the project.

But you, after your initial research, emphasize the importance of a good infrastructure that is built on Oracle WebLogic.

Because of the good and solid presentation of your research, you get the green light to go forward.

In the next chapter, we will focus on installing the Oracle WebLogic Server with its many options, examples, and demos. Have fun!

2
The Beginning: Planning and Installation

Congratulations! The management has given you the green light to proceed with Oracle WebLogic. So now you will have to arrange for some important things before you can start your first installation.

The first thing you do is go and talk to the Operating Systems Administration department to choose the right hardware and operating system, based on the specifications Oracle WebLogic needs.

Choosing your hardware

Choosing the right hardware is an important matter, but in most cases a company follows a strategy to decide what hardware should be used for what purpose.

Anyway, Oracle WebLogic is certified for several different hardware architectures; see the full list of certifications at:

http://www.oracle.com/technetwork/middleware/ias/downloads/fusion-
certification-100350.html.

- Minimum CPU required is 1 GHz, but that's the absolute minimum. It is better to start from 2.5 GHz, with dual- or quad-core architecture. Intel and non-Intel processors are both supported.
- It depends on what you will run on top of your WebLogic, but a good start is 3GB, considering the number of simultaneous users, sessions, and in-memory programs.

- Storage refers to local hard disk or external storage. For just a WebLogic Server, installing 2 GB is enough, but be aware that normally you have to install additional software afterwards and configure your WebLogic domain. Consider around 5 to 7 GB, and then you're on the safer side.

- Hardware or virtualized? Nowadays most companies use virtualization of hardware to reduce costs. Virtualization can be done on AIX (LPAR), Sun (LDOM), or VMware. For a long time, Oracle did not support virtualization, but now Oracle offers its own virtualization solutions, such as Oracle VM and Virtual Box.

Operating system

Oracle WebLogic is certified on various operating systems, such as:

- Linux versions, including as Redhat, Oracle Linux, and SLES
- Sun Solaris
- HP-UX
- AIX
- Windows 2000-2003-2008 Server, XP

For a complete list of certified operating systems, see the Certification Matrix at `http://www.oracle.com/technetwork/middleware/downloads/fmw-11gr1certmatrix.xls`.

In your case, you will choose Oracle Enterprise Linux version 5, which is somewhat similar to the Redhat version. You can download it from Oracle TechNet.

The rest of this chapter will focus on installing WebLogic on a Linux platform.

Other prerequisites

- There should be a dedicated operating system user as the local owner of the WebLogic Server software. The typical name would be oracle, assigned with the group oinstall.

- There should be some file prerequisites set for the user:

  File limits should be set in `/etc/security/limits.conf`

  ```
  # /etc/security/limits.conf
  #<domain> <type> <item> <value>
  weblogic hard nofile 4096
  weblogic soft nofile 4096
  ```

- On some Linux systems, the `/tmp` filesystem is of a very small size. If this is the case, ask your OS administrator to increase it or else choose your own directory. This can be accomplished by entering the following option on the command line, when you start the installation program:

```
-Djava.io.tmpdir=tmpdirpath
```

  Here, `tmpdirpath` is the full path of the directory that you want to designate as a temporary storage area for the installation program.

Preparing your installation

First you have to decide which kind of installer package you will have to use. There are several types of installers.

Different types of installers

The following types of WebLogic Server installers are available:

- **OS-specific package installer**: This type of installer is a self-extracting executable binary of the installation that includes the JDK's JRockit and Hotspot for the selected platform. The installer may be either an `.exe` file or a `.bin` file, depending on the selected platform.

- **Generic package installer**: This type of installer is a `.jar` file. It does not include the JRockit and Hotspot. You can use this type of installer on machines where Java is already installed. For AIX, you need the IBM JDK. These kinds of JDKs are also not pre-packaged by Oracle.

- **Upgrade installer**: Upgrade installers allow you to upgrade an existing WebLogic Server installation to the current patch release. For example, if you have WebLogic Server 10.3.0, 10.3.1, or 10.3.2 installed, you can use an upgrade installer to upgrade your installation to WebLogic Server 10.3.3. If a patch upgrade is available for your current WebLogic Server installation, you can download an upgrade installer from My Oracle Support.

- **Zip installer**: It is mainly for developers.

Depending on your platform, you will have to choose the OS-specific package installer (`.bin` or `.exe` file) or a generic package installer (`.jar` file). For all 64-bit operating system versions, only a generic installer is available.

Choosing your installation mode

There are three types of installation modes:

- **GUI mode**: This requires a graphical environment. If you do an install on your own PC, there's always a graphics card, but a headless server usually doesn't have one, so you login remotely from your own PC. In this case, you will have to forward the DISPLAY to your own PC.

- **Console mode**: It is the same as the GUI mode but does not need a graphical environment. Installation is done through a text-based console.

- **Silent mode**: You use this mode for scripted, automated installations.

The best way to do this is to first do a GUI installation to get familiar with the diverse options before using the other ones.

GUI-based installation for WLS 10.3.3

Depending on the kind of package you use, you will have to execute the installer, the binary, or the generic package, as the dedicated owner of the WebLogic Server software (see Prerequisites).

Binary: In this case, make it executable and run it:

```
chmod +x wls1033_linux32.bin
./ wls1033_linux32.bin
```

Generic: Generic jar file:

```
PATH=$JAVA_HOME/bin:$PATH
export PATH
java -jar wls1033_generic.jar
```

For your 64-bit environment:

```
java -d64 -jar wls1033_generic.jar
```

This will result in a pop-up splash screen from the Oracle Installer. If this does not happen, then the user might not be authorized to use XWindows. So you will have to type >xhost +x as user root.

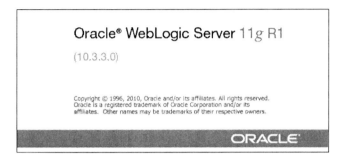

Since the installation process is pretty straightforward, let's run through the entire process. You were also asked to document all your steps for your colleagues. So now it's good to follow the several steps in the installation.

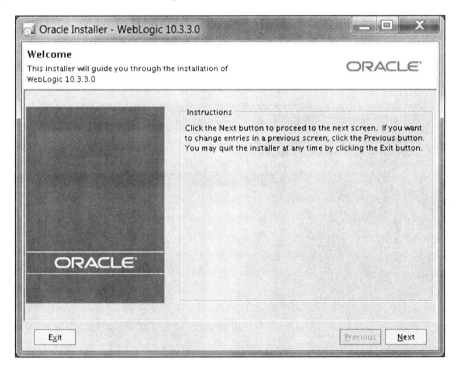

The first decision you will have to make is the name and location of your middleware home. This is the root-level of your WebLogic installation. One can follow many conventions, but keep it generic so that you can use it for all your environments.

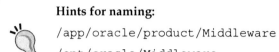

Hints for naming:

`/app/oracle/product/Middleware`

`/opt/oracle/Middleware`

`/u01/app/oracle/product/Middleware`

Considerations/best practices

- Do not include spaces in your pathnames, because the CLASSPATH might not be resolved because of a line break.

- Be aware of using capitals; Linux is case-sensitive.

- If you include version numbers, just use major release numbers, not small patches.

- Size your filesystems to be big enough; it gives you some space for increasing the capacity.

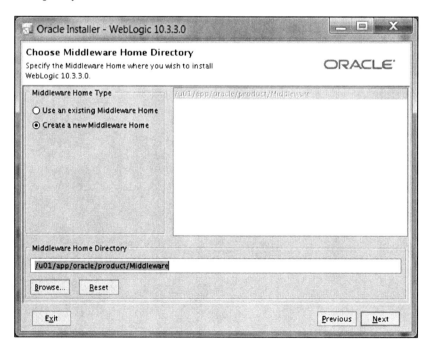

The directory will be created, but be aware that none of them exist and that you have enough permissions to write in it.

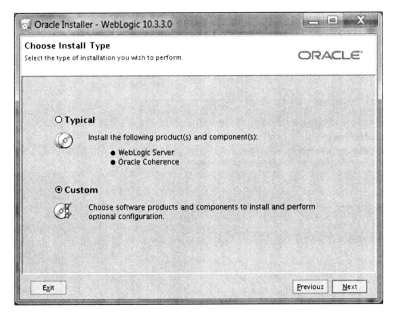

Choose the **Custom** option to see which options are available. In future, for silent installations you can script the components for your environment needs.

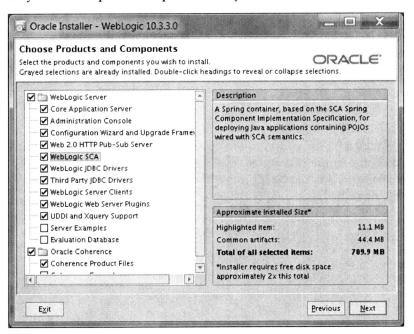

In the **Choose Products and Components** section, you see a list of components that you can select. Some are mandatory, such as the **Core Application Server**, others are optional, such as **WebLogic SCA** or **Oracle Coherence**. Depending on the applications you will run the top of your WebLogic Server, you will have to select or deselect components. For instance, Oracle SOA Suite requires WebLogic SCA, and for your Oracle Service Bus you want to implement Oracle Coherence, so think well about the purpose of your WebLogic Server.

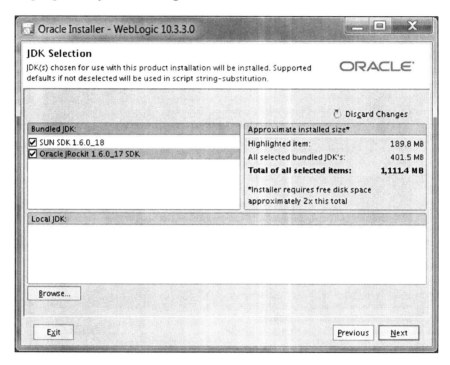

At WebLogic 10.3.3, there are still two Java environments available, SUN Hotspot and JRockit. Oracle prescribes using SUN Hotspot for Development Mode and JRockit for Production Mode. In earlier days, JRockit was dedicated to server environments and therefore performed better than the more client-based SUN Hotspot. But maybe it's more plausible to keep all environments equal (everywhere the same JDK).

For now, we run it in Development Mode so we choose SUN.

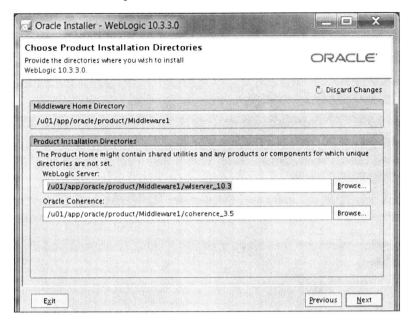

At this point, the WebLogic Server home directory for binaries, libraries, and configuration files is set. The other directories, such as in this example Oracle Coherence, will be set according to the additional components you chose before.

Then, an overview of the components and installation begins.

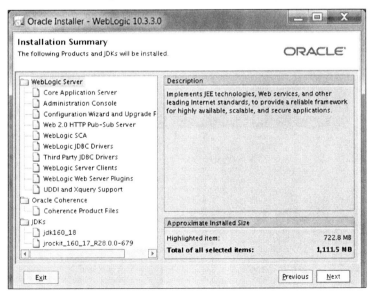

The installation summary gives you an overview of the components you have selected. Let's have a quick look at them and for the purposes they are used:

- **Core Application Server**: This is the complete WebLogic application server.
- **Administration Console**: The Administration Console application.
- **Configuration Wizard and Upgrade Framework**: This is the framework used for creating domains and performing upgrades.
- **Web 2.0 HTTP Pub-Sub Server**: This is the WebLogic's built-in HTTP Server.
- **WebLogic SCA**: This is a Spring container for Java applications that use the Service Component Architecture. This is included as an optional library in the WebLogic Server.
- **WebLogic JDBC Drivers and third-party JDBC Drivers**: These can be used to connect a WebLogic Server environment to an external database.

And some more options, such as cache memory Grid (Coherence) and a sample database.

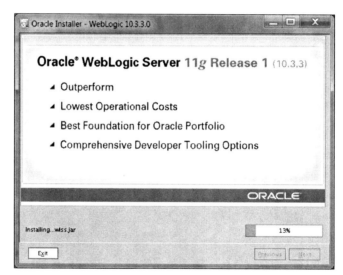

Then, an overview of the components and installation begins:

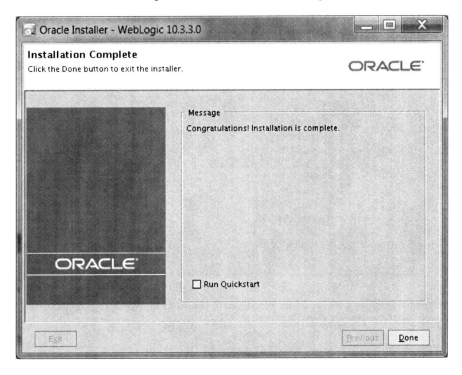

In the end, the QuickStart screen appears. You don't need to run that, so uncheck it.

QuickStart is designed to help first-time users evaluate, learn, and install a demo workshop. You could use this on your own personal computer.

Installation done

As you probably noticed, there is no rocket science involved. The installer is pretty straightforward. It's good, if you are a novice to WebLogic, to do the installation in this way. Thus, you become familiar with it, so when you're more experienced you can automate your installation (as will be discussed later in this chapter).

Now, the WebLogic software is installed but where do you find your files? Look at the overview in the following screenshot:

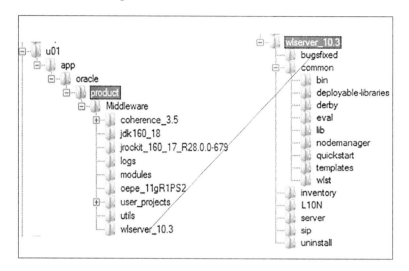

This filesystem path is just an example of how it could be installed, depending on the choices you made during installation.

Middleware Home-`/u01/app/oracle/product/Middleware`.

- `registry.dat`/`registry.xml`(not visible, but in oracle home directory): This is a record of all Oracle middleware products.
- `coherence_3.5`: This is in the memory Cache Datagrid.
- `jdk160_18`: This is Sun Java JDK.
- `jrocket_160_17_R28.0.0-679`: This is Oracle BEA Java JDK.
- `logs`: These are the Installation logs.
- `modules`: These are the Modules (`.jar`) installed in Oracle Home.
- `Oepe_11gR1PS2`: This is the Oracle Enterprise Pack for Eclipse that is the Development environment.
- `user_projects`: This is the default location for domains created by the user.
- `utils`: These are additional or utility JAR files.
- `wlserver_10.3`: This is the Oracle WebLogic Server 10.3.3 Home
- `common`: These are the files shared by the Oracle WebLogic Server 10.3.3 components, including the template JAR files used by the Configuration Wizard when creating domains.

- `Samples` (optional): These are sample code and resources.
- `server`: These include server software components (executables, database files, XML JAR files, alternative JDBC drivers, Oracle WebLogic Server JAR files, and plug-ins).
- `uninstall`: This is the code required to uninstall Oracle WebLogic Server 10.3.3.

Installation in console mode

An installation in console mode is quite similar to the GUI install, the only difference is that the screens will appear text-based. If you don't have your DISPLAY setting exported to your own desktop, it will appear when you choose the option console mode. The –mode=console redirects the output in text to your computer screen.

```
./wls1033_linux32.bin -mode=console

Extracting 0%..............................................................
........................................100%

<----------------------------------------------------------- Oracle
Installer - WebLogic 10.3.3.0 ---------------------------------------------
--------------->

Welcome:

--------

This installer will guide you through the installation of WebLogic
10.3.3.0. Type "Next" or enter to proceed to the next prompt.  If you
want to change data entered previously, type "Previous".  You may quit
the installer at any time by typing "Exit".

Enter [Exit] [Next] >

<----------------------------------------------------------- Oracle
Installer - WebLogic 10.3.3.0 ---------------------------------------------
--------------->

Choose Middleware Home Directory:

--------------------------------

 ->1|* Create a new Middleware Home
   2|/u01/app/oracle/product/Middleware
```

The rest of the installation is the same as the GUI installation, so there's no need to discuss this option any further.

Silent and scripted installation

After your first steps with the installation, you begin to wonder if it's possible to create a more permanent solution, which can be used in your company; in other words, how to automate your installation, because you will have to install a huge quantity of WebLogic servers.

Well, certainly there is a way! Oracle provides a silent installation, based on a XML template, which is used to specify the components you need.

What is a silent mode installation?

Silent mode can be used to specify your installation settings, and after you've set it you can propagate the same installation settings to multiple machines. During installation in silent mode, the installation program reads the settings for your configuration from an XML file that you create prior to beginning the installation. The installation program does not display any configuration options during the installation process. Silent-mode installation works on both Windows and UNIX systems.

With this, you can create a simple shell script or command file that sequentially runs silent mode installation and silent-mode configuration.

Silent installation: step by step

The silent installation has basically two steps:

Generating a silent XML file

There are samples available on OTN:

(http://download.oracle.com/docs/cd/E14571_01/doc.1111/e14142/silent. htm), so here's the sample. I have left out the comments:

```
<?xml version="1.0" encoding="UTF-8"?>
<!-- Silent installer option -mode=silent -
silent_xml=C:\myfiles\silent.xml -->
<?xml version="1.0" encoding="UFF-8"?>
  <bea-installer>
    <input-fields>
      <data-value name="BEAHOME" value="D:\Oracle\Middleware_Home" />
      <data-value name="WLS_INSTALL_DIR"
value="D:\Oracle\Middleware_Home\wlserver_10.3" />
```

```
        <data-value name="COMPONENT_PATHS"
            value="WebLogic Server/Core Application Server|WebLogic Server
/Administration Console|WebLogic Server/Configuration Wizard and
Upgrade
Framework|WebLogic Server/Web 2.0 HTTP Pub-Sub Server|WebLogic Server/
WebLogic
JDBC Drivers|WebLogic Server/Third Party JDBC Drivers|WebLogic Server
/WebLogic Server Clients|WebLogic Server/WebLogic Web Server Plugins
|WebLogic Server/UDDI and Xquery Support|WebLogic Server/Server
Examples|Oracle Coherence/Coherence Product Files" />
        <data-value name="INSTALL_NODE_MANAGER_SERVICE" value="yes" />
        <data-value name="NODEMGR_PORT" value="5559" />
        <data-value name="INSTALL_SHORTCUT_IN_ALL_USERS_FOLDER"
 value="yes"/>
    <!--
        <data-value name="LOCAL_JVMS"
 value="D:\jrockit_160_05|D:\jdk160_11"/>
    -->


    </input-fields>
  </bea-installer>
```

The values of local directories like BEAHOME and LOCAL_JVMS can be different on your system.

There are several values you have to be aware of:

- BEAHOME: The Middleware Home directory such as /u01/app/oracle/ Middleware.

- WLS_INSTALL_DIR: Complete pathname that is given to the product installation such as /u01/app/oracle Middleware/wlserver_10.3.

- COMPONENT_PATHS: Components and subcomponents that are to be installed.

  To install multiple components, separate the components with a pipe (|).To install subcomponents, specify a component/subcomponent combination by using the component; forward slash (/); subcomponent format.

- INSTALL_NODE_MANAGER_SERVICE: Installs Node Manager as a Windows service. The default is "no".

- NODEMGR_PORT: Specifies the Node Manager Listen port number. If not specified, it uses 5556.

- BEA_BUNDLED_JVMS: Option to select BEA bundled JVMS such as jrockit_160_05 or jdk160_05 for Windows and LinuxLOCAL_JVMS: Option to select supported JVM, which is already installed. This is when you use the generic jar installer, which doesn't include the Java install package.

You must be aware of choosing the right components. Here's an overview of the components:

Product/Component	Optional/Mandatory
WebLogic Server	Mandatory
Core Application Server	Mandatory
Administration Console	Mandatory
Configuration Wizard and Upgrade Framework	Mandatory
Web 2.0 HTTP Pub-Sub Server	Mandatory
Weblogic SCA	Optional, but mandatory addition Oracle Software
WebLogic JDBC Drivers	Mandatory
Third Party JDBC Drivers	Optional
WebLogic Server Clients	Optional
WebLogic Web Server Clients	Optional
WebLogic Web Server Plugins	Optional
UDDI and Xquery Support	Optional, but mandatory addition Oracle Software
Server Examples	Optional
Evaluation Database	Optional
Oracle Coherence	
Coherence Product Files	Optional
Coherence Examples	
Oracle Enterprise Pack for Eclipse	Only for server-side Eclipse IDE
Common files	

Running the silent installation

Because your company uses Linux and UNIX for server-side solutions, the way to do the installation on Linux is discussed here, and on Windows it will be quite similar.

1. Go to the directory that contains the installation program. On a Linux 32-bit environment, this will be `wls1033_linux32.bin`. When you install with the generic jar installer, it will be `wls1033_generic.jar`.

2. Launch the installation program by entering the following commands:

```
chmod a+x wls1033_linux32.bin
./wls1033_linux32.bin -mode=silent -silent_xml=path_to_silent.xml
```

Or use the generic installer:

```
java -jar wls1033_generic.jar -mode=silent -
silent_xml=path_to_silent.xml
```

On a 64-bit environment use the –d64 option, such as `java –d64 –jar....`

`path_to_silent.xml`, which is the full path of the silent.xml file.

Some additional options you can add are `-log=path_to_logfile`.

Using a pre-installed Java home

The generic installer does not include a JAVA installer. In this case, you can use the native operating system JAVA or install the package yourself.

If you have installed the package, you will have to give the option:

```
-jreLoc=<location of your JAVA installation>
```

Exit codes

The installation can end with 3 different exit codes:

- `0`: Successful installation.
- `1`: Installation failed due to a fatal error.

  Could be a missing directory or missing permissions to the file locations, which you specified in your XML.
- `2`: Installation failed due to an internal XML parsing error.

  This is normally a typo or a missing quote in your XML files.

  ```
  ** Error during execution, error code = 65280"
  ```

Scripted installations

The use of the XML template enables you to script your installation with a shell script (on Linux/UNIX) or batch script (on Windows).

In this shell script, you can specify the same options you use when doing an installation from the command-line.

With scripted installation, you can automate your installation. You can even ask your Linux administrator to run the script during the creation of the Linux environment. So in this case, you provide them the necessary software and template, and they can deliver you a completely installed WebLogic Server.

Summary

So, your first steps into the wondrous world of Oracle WebLogic have been a success. Your boss came to your desk, stood beside you, and you told him all the secrets you know about what needs to be done during installations. He got confused and lost when you began talking about silent installs and said, "Yeah, yeah, it's ok", and walked away, impatient as he is.

You have set the basis for your WebLogic environments. With your scripted installations, the OS admins are now busy running it on about 20 machines, which are going to be used for several different applications.

But actually, this is just the beginning, and you know that. Because after the software is installed, you will come to a more difficult part, doing the WebLogic Domain configuration.

3
Oracle WebLogic Software Installed; What's Next?

In the previous chapter, you've managed to install the Oracle WebLogic Server software and discovered its different options, such as the GUI, the console, and the silent installation.

You are now busy making automated installation for your company based on scripts and XML templates for the various environments that are going to be used.

Your boss got inspired by you, and began installing his own WebLogic. One day, with sweat on his forehead, he came out of his office, and yelled, "My WebLogic installation has been successful!!" When you entered his office you saw that he was right. But now, he asked, "What's next?"

That's a good question…what's next?

The next steps

Of course, you knew that only installing the software wouldn't be enough. Now the configuration part has to take place. This next step that you will have to take can be done in two ways:

- If you use your Oracle WebLogic with another product from the Oracle product stack, such as Oracle SOA Suite, Oracle WebCenter, or Oracle Service Bus, you will have to install this software before domain creation.

- If not, you can continue and follow the steps that are involved in creating a domain.

The WebLogic domain

Firstly, it is a good thing to understand some concepts of Oracle WebLogic. For instance, what is a WebLogic domain? What is an administration server and what does it do?

A WebLogic domain is the bundled administration unit in which a WebLogic Server performs its tasks. Bundled in here are all kinds of tasks, such as leveraging applications, providing security, database access, tools, and much more.

A domain is a logically related group of Weblogic Servers that are managed as a unit. A central Weblogic Server, called the administration server, acts as the coordinator and is responsible for the management of the domain.

All other server instances except the Administration Server Instance are called Managed Server Instances. You usually deploy your applications in them.

A domain may also include WebLogic Server Clusters. Clusters are groups of WebLogic Servers that work together to provide scalability and high-availability for applications.

A minimal domain can contain only one WebLogic Server instance, which always functions as an Administration Server, but at the same time could be acting as a Managed Server. This could be the case when you are on a development system, but is not recommended for use in a production environment.

The following diagram shows a simple WebLogic domain configuration:

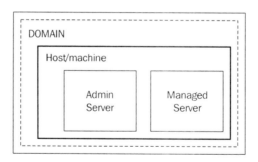

Before discussing the various components of a WebLogic domain, let's first create one!

Creating and configuring a domain

We'll first start with a simple domain without cluster or any Managed Server. This is the simplest way. I'd rather like to recommend creating at least one Managed Server Instance. The extra effort needed is minimal.

The following steps need to be followed while configuring a working domain:

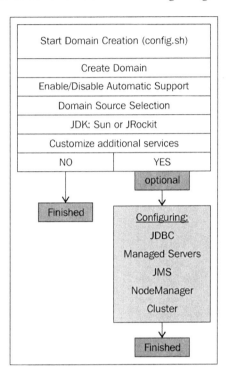

This is a schematic overview about how a domain is created:

- The first step to take is to run the `config.sh` (*NIX) or `config.bat` (Windows). In a default WebLogic installation, (with no additional software, such as the SOA Suite or any other product installed) you can find it in the Middleware home, `wlserver_10.3/common/bin`.

- The Middleware home depends on how you specified it during installation; it could be something such as `/u01/app/oracle/product/Middleware`.

- You can choose two modes: GUI or console. For this, we will use the GUI mode.

- WLST: You can create offline domains with the WebLogic Scripting Tool using templates.

  After executing the `config.sh` the screen appears similar to the following screenshot:

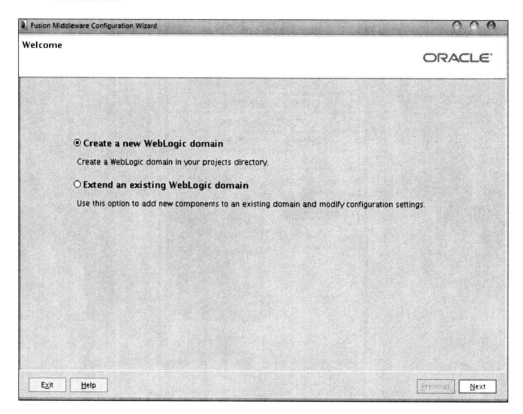

- Click **Next** to proceed.

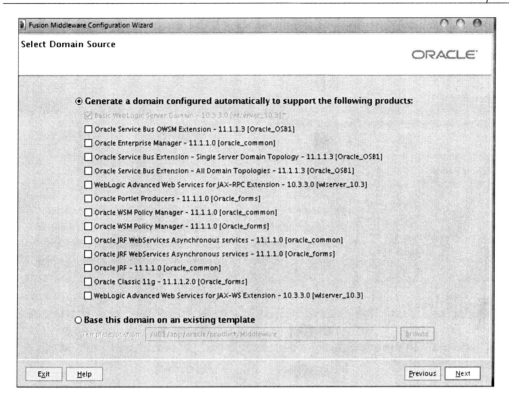

Depending on the purpose of your domain, you can add software. For a simple domain, the base template is already selected. This base template, `wls.jar` is shipped with your WebLogic software, in the WebLogic Server Home, `/common/templates`.

Selection of the necessary options depends on the purpose for which your WebLogic Server will be used. The templates will be discussed later in this chapter.

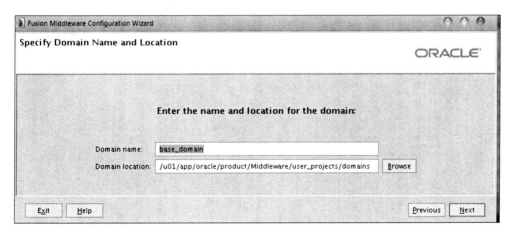

You can fill in the name of your domain, as shown in the previous screenshot. Try to think of a smart name, such as the purpose for which it will be used. For instance when you use the domain for some finance applications, it could be called the finance_domain.

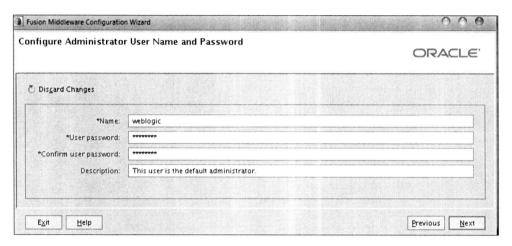

You have to fill in the administrator's username and password, as shown in the previous screenshot:

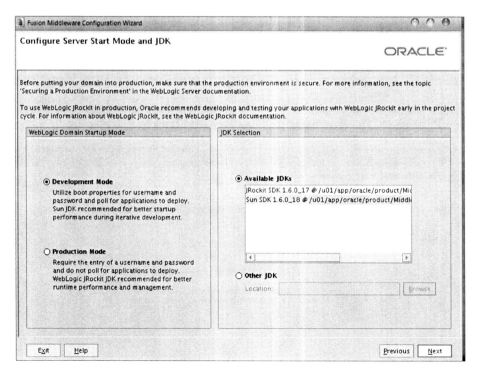

As shown in the previous screenshot, you have two options:

- **Development Mode** or **Production Mode**: The choice seems to be obvious. In production, you of course choose the Production Mode, but for the other stages you can choose either Development or Production Mode.

- For Production Mode you choose JRockit and for Development Mode you choose SUN Hotspot. This is recommended by Oracle.

Different modes explained

In order to choose between Development Mode and Production Mode, please be aware of the following points:

- **Stricter security policy**: In Production Mode, there will be a stricter security policy at the server level. This means that a file called `boot.properties`, which contains the encrypted administrator username and password, is not automatically generated. This is used to start up your WebLogic domain for authenticating the Administrator.

- **Automatic deployment**: Automatic deployment of an application is enabled in Development Mode. So when you drop an application in a specific directory, it is automatically deployed by WebLogic Server. This is something that you would not want the default behavior to be in a production environment. In Production Mode, by default, this is switched off.

- **Debugging**: This is disabled by default in Production whereas in Development Mode it is enabled. The reason is apparent, since you usually do not do debugging in production because of the performance impact.

- **JDK: Prod Mode: JRockit, Dev Mode: Sun**: For development it does not matter what you choose, but for production it could be interesting to look at JRockit. It claims to be a very fast JVM with predictable performance. So when real-time hiccups are not wanted because of garbage collection, it might be interesting to look at JRockit. You have some more capabilities for real-time processing through smarter garbage collection. JRockit mission control gives good insight into JVM performance and other statistics.

As shown in the following screenshot, you can select optional components to configure, such as names of Managed Server instances and locations of JMS file stores. This could be a smart move, if you want to configure your domain with other than the default settings.

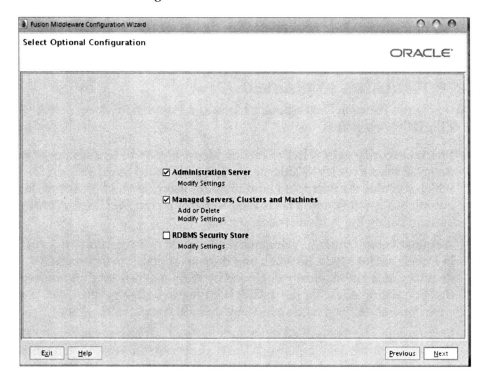

In the next section, you can configure some items such as the Administration Servers and Managed Servers.

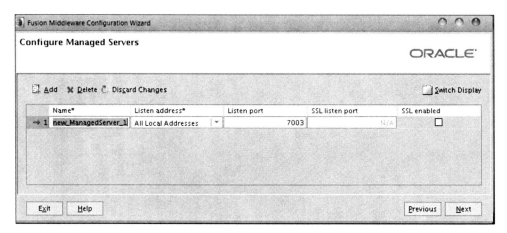

1. Configure the hostname as the Listen address and choose any available port. Managed Servers will be discussed later on in this book.

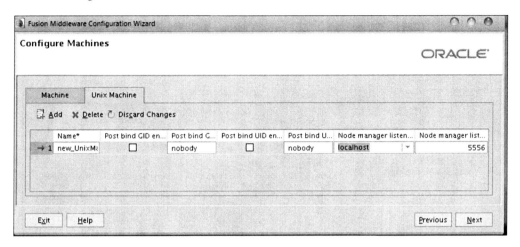

2. You should configure a machine for your Node Manager configuration.

   The Node Manager concept will be covered in *Chapter 5, Managed Servers and Node Manager*.

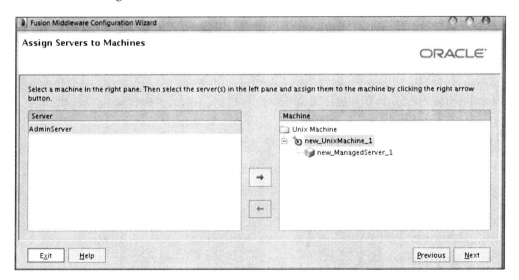

3. To use the Node Manager with your Admin and Managed Servers, place them under the machine name. The deeper meanings of this will be discussed in *Chapter 5, Managed Servers and Node Manager*.

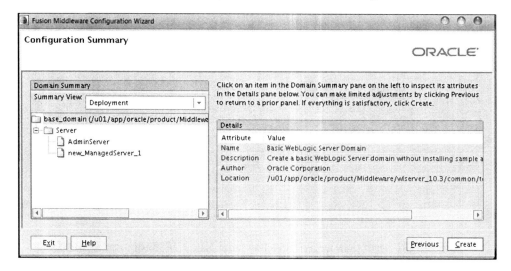

4. Review and click **Create**.

Well, that was pretty easy, wasn't it? Now your domain will be created. As I mentioned before, it is better to walk through the GUI mode to get familiar with all kinds of topics, so later on we can get into the details.

After the creation of your domain is done, you now have to start it in order to login into the Administration Console. But before continuing, let's explain a few things.

The domain's directory structure

By creating a domain, you define a collection of resources, such as:

- Managed Servers
- Clusters
- Database connections
- Security services
- Java EE applications

After the domain has been created, some files and directories are placed on your local server. Let's take a look:

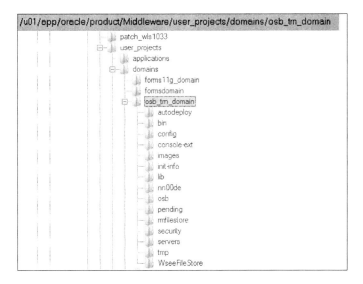

- `domain-name`: The name of this directory is the name of the domain.
- `autodeploy`: In development mode, WLS automatically deploys any applications or modules that you place in this directory. This directory provides a quick way to deploy applications in a development server. When the Oracle WebLogic Server instance runs in development mode, it automatically deploys any applications or modules that are placed in this directory.
- `bin`: This directory contains the scripts that are used for starting and stopping the Administration Server and the Managed Servers in the domain. These scripts are generally provided as `.sh` files for UNIX and `.cmd` files for Windows. The `bin` directory can optionally contain other scripts of domain-wide interest, such as scripts to start and stop database management systems, full-text search engine processes, and so on.
- `config`: The current configuration and deployment state of the domain is stored into the configuration repository, represented as the `config.xml`. All configurations in WebLogic are stored as xml files in this directory. When the Admin Server boots, it reads this file and knows how its domain is configured. Managed Servers also use this configuration for their part/role within the domain.

- `console-ext`: This directory contains extensions to the Administration Console, which enables you to add content to Oracle WebLogic Server Administration Console, replace content, and change the logos, styles, and colors without modifying the files that are installed with Oracle WebLogic Server. For example, you can add content that provides custom monitoring and management facilities for your applications.

- `init-info`: This directory contains files that are used for WebLogic domain provisioning. You should not modify any files in this directory.

- `lib`: Any JAR files that you put in this directory are added to the Java system `CLASSPATH` of each server instance in the domain when the server's Java Virtual Machine starts.

- `pending`: This directory contains the domain configuration files that represent the configuration changes that have been requested, but not yet been activated. After the configuration changes are activated, the configuration files are deleted from this directory. Configurations can be changed at runtime in the console of the Administration Server. Before they are implemented within the domain, they are temporarily stored in this directory.

- `security`: This directory holds the security-related files that are same for every Oracle WebLogic Server instance in the domain: `SerializedSystemIni.dat`.It also holds the security-related files that are needed only by the domain's Administration Server:
  - `DefaultAuthorizerInit.ldift`
  - `DefaultAuthenticatorInit.ldift`
  - `DefaultRoleMapperInit.ldift`

- `servers`: The server's directory that contains the subdirectories for the Administration and Managed Servers is created the first time the servers are started. This directory contains one subdirectory for each Oracle WebLogic Server instance in the domain. The subdirectories contain data that is specific to each server instance.

- `tmp`: This directory is used for temporarily storing files. You should not modify any files in this directory.

- `user_staged_config`: This directory is an alternative to the `config` directory, if the domain is set up such that the configuration information is "user-staged".

Domain creation explained: Domain templates

A domain is created based on a template. This template is a JAR (JAVA Archive) and it contains all the necessary components to create a simple WebLogic domain. The file is called `wls.jar` and is located in the WebLogic Server home under `common/templates/domains` after installation.

Different types of templates

The types of template include:

1. Domain template: It defines the full set of resources within a domain, including infrastructure components, applications, services, security options, and general environment and operating system options. The product installation includes a predefined Basic WebLogic Server Domain template. This template defines the core set of resources within a domain, including an Administration Server and basic configuration information.

2. Extension template: It defines the applications and services that you can add to an existing domain, such as the Enterprise Manager, ADF Runtime libraries, or templates shipped in other Oracle products. The extension templates are located in the WebLogic Server home, `common/templates/applications`.

Contents of the basic WLS template, `wls.jar`, are shown in the following screenshot:

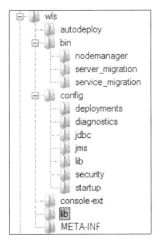

The pack command

One of the ways to create or use a template is the pack command (`pack.sh/cmd`).

The `pack` and `unpack` commands provide a simple, one-step method for creating domains and templates from the command line.

These shell scripts are available in `$MW_HOME/wlserver_[ver]/common/bin`.

Syntax of the `pack` command:

```
WL_HOME/common/bin/pack.sh -managed=true -domain=DOMAIN_PATH
-template=DOMAIN_TEMPLATE -template_name=DOMAIN_TEMPLATE_NAME
```

Syntax of the `unpack` command:

```
WL_HOME/common/bin/unpack.sh -domain=DOMAIN_PATH -template=DOMAIN_
TEMPLATE
```

You would also need `pack` and `unpack` commands to run a **Managed Server** on a machine that is remote from the **Administration Server** for the domain.

It is best to follow the procedure given next:

1. First create the domain on the node of the Administration Server.
2. Initiate the `pack` command with the necessary options.
3. Transfer the domain jar file to the second node.
4. First install the Oracle WebLogic software here, and then unpack the domain. Use the same directory structure as on the first node, to have equally configured environments.

When packing a domain that contains Managed Servers, you should use the `managed server=true` option.

Other ways of domain creation

In the previous sections, we discussed domain creation through GUI, but there are some other ways to create a domain as well.

Console-based domain creation

On `*nix`-like systems, there is usually no graphical environment available. You can solve this by exporting the GUI to your local desktop, with an XClient, such as XVNC or XMing, but if you don't do it or you give the option `mode=console`, you get a text-based representation of your GUI installation.

```
./config.sh mode=console
```

The output will be:

```
<----------------------------------------------------- BEA WebLogic
Configuration Wizard -------------------------------------------------
---->
Welcome: --------
Choose between creating and extending a domain. Based on your
selection, the Configuration Wizard guides you through the steps to
generate a new or extend an existing domain.
1|Create a new WebLogic domain
   | Create a WebLogic domain in your projects directory.
2|Extend an existing WebLogic domain
   | Extend an existing WebLogic domain.  Use this option to add
applications and services, or to override existing database access
   |(JDBC) and messaging (JMS) settings. You can also incorporate
additional functionality in your domain, for example, by including
   |AquaLogic Service Bus.



Enter index number to select OR [Exit][Next]> 1



<--------------- BEA WebLogic Configuration Wizard --------------->
Select Domain Source:
---------------------
Select the source from which the domain will be created. You can
create the domain by selecting from the required components or by
selecting from a list of existing domain templates.
1|Choose Weblogic Platform components
   | You can choose the Weblogic component(s) that you want supported
in your domain.
2|Choose custom template
   | Choose this option if you want to use an existing template. This
could be a custom created template using the Template Builder.



Enter index number to select OR [Exit][Previous][Next]> 1



<--------------- BEA WebLogic Configuration Wizard --------------->
Application Template Selection:
------------------------------

  Available Templates
    |_____WebLogic Server (Required)x
```

```
Enter number exactly as it appears in brackets to toggle selection OR
[Exit][Previous][Next]> 1


<--------------- BEA WebLogic Configuration Wizard --------------->
Application Template Selection:
-----------------------------

  Available Templates
  |_____WebLogic Server (Required)x
   ** Invalid input, not selectable
Enter number exactly as it appears in brackets to toggle selection OR
[Exit][Previous][Next]>

...--> and so on.
```

The procedure will be exactly the same as with the GUI.

Domain creation with the WebLogic Scripting Tool (WLST)

Although WLST will be discussed later on in *Chapter 13, WLST Makes an Administrator's Life Easier*, let's take a sneak peek into the possibilities it has for you.

WLST is a scripting language which is based on the Python programming language. Because the WebLogic Domain software is JAVA-based, you will need the JAVA implementation of Python, which is called Jython. In fact this is where WLST does its work.

The following script is a very simple WLST script to create a WebLogic domain:

```
#==============================================================
# Create a domain from the weblogic domain template.
#==============================================================
readTemplate('/u01/app/oracle/product/Middleware/common/templates/
domains/wls.jar')
cd('Servers/AdminServer')
#==============================================================
# Configure the Administration Server
#==============================================================
set('ListenAddress',''WLADMINIP'')
set('ListenPort', 9913)
```

```
#=================================================================
# Define the password for user weblogic. You must define the password
before you
# can write the domain.
#=================================================================
cd('/')
cd('Security/base_domain/User/weblogic')
cmo.setPassword(AdminServerPassword)

# - OverwriteDomain:Overwrites domain when saving
setOption('OverwriteDomain', 'true')


#==============================================================
# Write the domain, close the domain template and exit from the WLST
#==============================================================
writeDomain('/u01/app/oracle/product/Middleware/user_projects/
domains/wlsdom')
closeTemplate()
exit()
```

Be aware, that this is a very basic domain creation. If you create more advanced domains, such as a domain for the Oracle SOA suite, you should use more and more options to successfully create your domain, such as configuring JDBC, JMS, Resource adapters, and so on. This book is not about that, but perhaps in the future it may be included in an advanced version on WebLogic administration.

Server and domain start scripts

To run Oracle WebLogic Server *itself*, PATH and CLASSPATH environment variables are usable without any additional modification. Environment variables are set properly in start scripts, which call the setWLSEnv.sh script. The setWLSEnv.sh script is shipped with the WebLogic Server software.

The setWLSEnv script sets some WebLogic Server-specific settings, such as server CLASSPATH.

Start scripts and domain scripts are created during installation. It's possible to modify the start scripts' environment variables based on deployed applications' requirements. These start and domain scripts are created in the Domain directory, under /bin.

The scripts are:

- `setDomainEnv.sh`: This script is used to set up all the environment variables and Java options required to run WebLogic Server, in the WebLogic Integration domain. It also calls the `setWLSEnv.sh` from the WebLogic Server home.

- `startWeblogic.sh`: This script is used to start the WebLogic Domain along with the Admin Server.

- `stopWeblogic.sh`: This script is used to stop the WebLogic Domain entirely.

- `startManagedWeblogic.sh`: This script is used to start a Managed Server instance from the command line.

- `stopManagedWeblogic.sh`: This script is used to stop a Managed Server instance from the command line.

An important configuration file: config.xml

When a domain is created, all the main basic configuration regarding the WebLogic Domain is stored in a file called `config.xml`. This file is stored under the WebLogic Domain directory, in the `config` directory.

The `config.xml` file consists of a series of XML elements. The Domain element is the top-level element, and all the other elements in the Domain are children of the Domain element. The Domain element includes child elements, such as the Server, Cluster, and Application elements. These child elements may have children themselves.

Editing the `config.xml` manually is not recommended, but if you do, you should edit it only when the WebLogic Domain is completely down, because it gets updated frequently during runtime.

The following is an example of a part of the `config.xml`:

```xml
<?xml version='1.0' encoding='UTF-8'?>
<domain xmlns="http://xmlns.oracle.com/weblogic/domain"
xmlns:sec="http://xmlns.oracle.com/weblogic/security"
xmlns:wls="http://xmlns.oracle.com/weblogic/security/
wls" xmlns:xsi="http://www.w3.org/2001/XMLSchema-instance"
xsi:schemaLocation="http://xmlns.oracle.com/weblogic/security/xacml
http://xmlns.oracle.com/weblogic/security/xacml/1.0/xacml.xsd http://
xmlns.oracle.com/weblogic/security/providers/passwordvalidator http://
xmlns.oracle.com/weblogic/security/providers/passwordvalidator/1.0/
passwordvalidator.xsd http://xmlns.oracle.com/weblogic/domain http://
xmlns.oracle.com/weblogic/1.0/domain.xsd http://xmlns.oracle.com/
weblogic/security http://xmlns.oracle.com/weblogic/1.0/security.xsd
```

```
http://xmlns.oracle.com/weblogic/security/wls http://xmlns.oracle.com/
weblogic/security/wls/1.0/wls.xsd">
  <name>base_domain</name>
  <domain-version>10.3.3.0</domain-version>
  <security-configuration>
    <name>base_domain</name>
    <realm>
      <sec:authentication-provider xsi:type="wls:default-
authenticatorType">
```

....

```
    <name>base_domain</name>
    <file-name>/u01/app/oracle/product/Middleware/logs/osb_trn_domain/
osb_trn_domain.log</file-name>
    <rotation-type>none</rotation-type>
  </log>
  <server>
    <name>AdminServer</name>
    <log>
      <name>AdminServer</name>
      <date-format-pattern>MMM d, yyyy h:mm:ss a z</date-format-
pattern>
      <file-name>/u01/app/oracle/product/Middleware/logs/osb_trn_
domain/AdminServer.log</file-name>
      <rotation-type>none</rotation-type>
```

....

All configurable items that you can change end up here. Some deeper configuration items, such as JDBC and JMS, only have a top-level in the `config.xml` and a shortcut to their own configuration file.

For instance, when you configure a JDBC datasource named `dataSource1`, a file is created in the domain `config/jdbc` directory, usually named as `dataSource1NNNN.xml`.

In your `config.xml`, the following section will appear:

```
<jdbc-system-resource>
    <name>dataSource1</name>
    <target>AdminServer,ms1</target>
    <descriptor-file-name>jdbc/dataSource1-jdbc.xml</descriptor-file-
name>
  </jdbc-system-resource>
  <jdbc-system-resource>
```

WebLogic Domain restrictions

In designing your domain configuration, note the following restrictions:

- Each domain requires its own Administration Server for performing management activities.

- All Managed Servers in a cluster must reside in the same domain; you cannot split a cluster over multiple domains.

- All Managed Servers in a domain must run the same version of the WebLogic server software. The Administration Server may run either the same version as the Managed Servers in the domain, or a latest service pack.

- If you have created multiple domains, each domain must have its own database schema (if needed). For example, if you create a JDBC data source in one domain, you cannot use it with a Managed Server or cluster in another domain. Instead, you must create a similar data source in the second domain. Furthermore, two or more system resources cannot have the same name.

Other Domain resources

Besides the Administration Server and Managed Servers, a domain also contains the resources and services that Managed Servers and deployed applications can use in order to function properly.

Managed Servers can use the following components or resources:

- **Machine definitions** that identify a particular physical piece of hardware. A machine definition is used to associate a physical host with the Managed Servers it hosts. This information is used by Node Manager in restarting a failed Managed Server, and by a clustered Managed Server in selecting the best location for storing replicated session data.

- **Network channels** that define default ports, protocols, and protocol settings that a Managed Server uses to communicate with clients. After creating a network channel, you can assign it to any number of Managed Servers and clusters in the domain. You can configure whether a channel supports outgoing connections or not. You can independently configure network traffic for client connections and server connections, and physically separate client and server network traffic onto different listen addresses or listen ports. You can also use channels on a Managed Server to support different protocols.

- **Virtual hosting**, which defines a set of hostnames to which WebLogic Server instances (servers) or clusters respond. When you use virtual hosting, you use DNS to specify one or more hostnames that map to the IP address of a server or cluster. You also specify which Web applications are served by each virtual host.

Applications can use the following resources and services:

- Security providers, which are components that handle specific aspects of security, such as authentication and authorization, certificates, and digital certificates.

- Resource adapters and connection factories, which are system libraries specific to Enterprise Information Systems (EIS) and provide connectivity to an EIS.

- Diagnostics and monitoring services.

- JDBC data sources, which enable applications to connect to databases.

- Mail sessions.

- XML entity caches and registry of XML parsers and transformer factories.

- Messaging services such as JMS servers and store-and-forward services.

- Persistent store, which is a physical repository for storing data, such as persistent JMS messages. It can either be a JDBC-accessible database or a disk-based file.

- Startup classes, which are Java programs that you create to provide custom, system-wide services for your applications.

- Work Managers, which determine how an application prioritizes the execution of its work based on rules that you define and by monitoring actual run-time performance. You can create Work Managers for the entire WebLogic Server domains or for specific application components.

- Work Contexts, which enable applications to pass properties to a remote context without including the properties in a remote call.

- Clustering, to Failover and Loadbalance applications.

Summary

So, you are already far ahead on the exciting road called Oracle WebLogic. You did your domain creation several times and with different options, and now you're ready to go on and start with some basic operation control tasks. One point of discussion within your FinanceFiction organization is whether or not to cluster and use failover.

Some of the FF applications that will be hosted later on the Oracle WebLogic platform will be highly critical and will require 24/7 availability.

We'll come to that later. You created the first domain for your development department, documented all the steps that you took, and now you are ready to go on to the next stage that is Operational Tasks.

4
Getting in Control: Operation Basics

Today you finally managed to get it done! It's time for your first demonstration of the project. As we've seen in the previous chapters, you've installed and configured your first WebLogic Server. Time for champagne! Or is it too early?

Getting started: Start your WebLogic domain

Before you can use the WebLogic Server, you first will have to start it. There are several options to start it, listed as follows:

- Using a start script, provided with the domain creation. On UNIX it's called `startWebLogic.sh`, on Windows `startWeLogic.cmd`
- On Windows, via the **Start** Menu
- With the WebLogic Scripting Tool (WLST)
- With the `java weblogic.Server` command

Using the startup script (startWebLogic)

The `startWebLogic` script does the following:

- Sets environment variables by invoking `DOMAIN_NAME/bin/setDomainEnv.sh` (`setDomainEnv.cmd` on Windows), where `DOMAIN_NAME` is the directory in which you located the domain.

- Invokes the `java weblogic.Server` command, which starts a JVM that is configured to run a WebLogic Server instance. When the server successfully completes its startup process, it writes the following message to standard out (which, by default, is the command window):

```
<Notice> <WebLogicServer> <BEA-000360> <Server started in
  RUNNING mode>
```

Or if it fails, you will get the following message:

```
Critical><WebLogicServer>….<BEA-000362><Server failed. Reason: …
stackdump

                      or ******************************************
********************************
The WebLogic Server did not start up properly.
Exception raised: Name Exception + some details
See preceding log message for details.
*****************************************************************
******
```

The startWebLogic script can be found in the Domain directory. This one invokes the real one, which is under `/bin` in the Domain directory.

When you issue the script on Linux, it's started in the foreground; that means if you terminate the shell 44 or logout, your WebLogic shuts down also.

A better way of starting on Linux is using the `nohup` in combination with the script.

A good option is:

```
nohup ./startWebLogic.sh > /dev/null &2>1
```

Where `nohup` gives a sign to the process to run even if the user logon (Operating System user of the WebLogic installation) gets terminated. Be aware to start it is as the owner of the WebLogic software, or at least with enough permissions to start/stop.

The `> /dev/null &2>1` is used to redirect the `STDOUT`, and `STDERR` into `/dev/null`, a sort of trash within Linux.

Using the java weblogic.Server command

Using this command can only be executed when running your WebLogic Server in development mode, because other than the start-scripts, it does not recognize patch levels, server environments, and so on.

First you set your environment with `<WL_HOME>/server/bin/setWLSEnv.sh`. Then run the command:

```
java weblogic.Server
```

Usually, run `java weblogic.Server` with some additional options, as seen in the following block of code:

```
java -server -Xms256m -Xmx512m -classpath "CLASSPATH"
  -Dweblogic.Name=SERVER_NAME
  -Dplatform.home=<WL_HOME>
  -Dweblogic.management.username=WLS_USER
  -Dweblogic.management.password=WLS_PW
  -Djava.security.policy= <WL_HOME>/server/lib/weblogic.policy
  weblogic.Server
```

Using the Windows Start menu

When you configured a WebLogic domain on Windows using the configuration wizard, the start script was made available on the start menu.

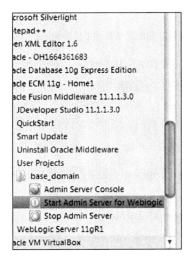

This is in fact the `startWebLogic.cmd` startup file, and shortcuts have been made for the domain start and stop scripts in the Windows Start menu.

Using WLST with and without Node Manager

Although WLST and the Node Manager will be discussed in *Chapter 13, WLST: Makes an Administrator's Life Easier* and *Chapter 5, Managed Servers and the Node Manager*, we can have a short overview here, on how to control your environment using these features.

WLST is a tool based on the Python programming language, for WebLogic used to access configurable items programmatically, so also stopping and starting the environment. If you have a lot of WebLogic environments to control, you can automate these with WLST to do some tasks for you; that is, it is practical to automate all the operational activities for production environments as the developers will not be involved in production operational activities. It is ideal for the support team or operational team that will maintain the environment; as said, it will be discussed in *Chapter 13, WLST: Makes an Administrator's Life Easier*.

Here is an example of starting WebLogic in WLST without the Node Manager.

First run the following code:

```
<WL_HOME>/common/bin/wlst.sh à this will set your environment setting
    for using WLST to connect to the WebLogic domain and starts the
    actual WLST prompt. WL_HOME is the WebLogic Server home directory.
```

Then, when the offline WLST prompt appears, type the following block of code:

```
wls:offline/>
startServer('AdminServer','mydomain','t3://localhost:7001',
    'weblogic','weblogic','<WL_DOMAIN_DIR>','true')
```

The following is an example of how to start using the Node Manager:

* Start Node Manager (for more details, see *Chapter 5, Managed Servers and the Node Manager*)

* Connect WLST to Node Manager

```
nmConnect('weblogic', 'weblogic', 'localhost',
    '5556','mydomain','<WL_DOMAIN_DIR>')
```

Now, start the Administration Server:

```
wls:/nm/mydomain>nmStart('AdminServer')
```

Starting other servers using the WebLogic Admin console

When the WebLogic Administration Server has been started, all other WebLogic Managed Server instances (for more on Managed Servers, see *Chapter 5, Managed Servers and the Node Manager*) can be started using the Administration Console. This is only possible if the Node Manager is started and running on the specific host. On the control tab of the servers, you can find the **Stop** and **Start** buttons. For more information about how to use the Administration Console, have a look at *Ease of use: the Administration Console* section later in this chapter.

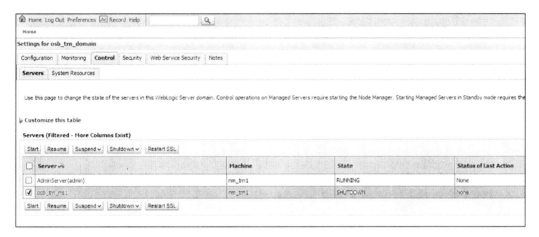

Things to know before starting up for the first time

If you start up your WebLogic for the first time, there are some important things to know:

Boot identity issues

Are you starting up in Development or Production mode? When starting up in Production mode, the first time it will fail: the server will not startup if the `boot.properties` file is not present. However, WebLogic will ask on the console for the user/password for the admin user. You can also specify the user/password in the script/command line.

- This is because the startup requires some security/identity parameters, stored in a file called `boot.properties`. This will give an entry in the logs.

- This file contains the username and password of the WebLogic Admin user, and is stored in the `<WL_DOMAIN_DIR>/servers/AdminServer/security`.

- However, the first time you startup, this directory has not been created yet, so you will have to accept the first time startup failure. After the failure you create the directory security under `<WL_DOMAIN_DIR>/servers/AdminServer`, and create a file named `boot.properties`. Of course, you also could perform this action before starting.

- Content of the `boot.properties` file:

```
username=<name of WebLogic Admin ( usually weblogic)>
password=<password>
```

- Now save this file and issue the startup sequence again. The contents of the `boot.properties` file will now be encrypted, upon successful startup.

Using java weblogic.Server command to create a Boot Identity file

Besides creating the file on the OS, you can also create it with the `java weblogic.Server` command.

For example, the following command starts an Administration Server named `myAdminServer` and creates a boot identity file:

```
java -Dweblogic.management.username=weblogic
   -Dweblogic.management.password=welcome1
   -Dweblogic.system.StoreBootIdentity=true
   -Dweblogic.Name=myAdminServer weblogic.Server
```

Alternative to boot.properties

In case you don't want to use the `boot.properties` file or enter the username/password during server startup, and if security is not a concern, you can add the following values in the server startup script.

```
-Dweblogic.management.username=username
-Dweblogic.management.password=password
```

Like in `startWeblogic.sh`:

```
-Dweblogic.management.username=<weblogic username>
-Dweblogic.management.password=<weblogic password>
```

However, keeping clear-text passwords is not a very good practice.

You can create the `boot.properties` file by keeping the following values in the startup script:

```
-Dweblogic.management.username=username
-Dweblogic.management.password=password
-Dweblogic.system.StoreBootIdentity=true
```

This will create a `boot.properties` file under the `AdminServer/security` directory.

Once the file is generated and in case you don't want to keep clear-text passwords in startup scripts, you can remove the added options.

Keeping boot.properties at user-defined location

The `boot.properties` file can be placed at a user-defined location by keeping the following flag in startup script:

```
-Dweblogic.system.BootIdentityFile=filename
```

With this option, `boot.properties` file can be renamed with some other name such as:

```
-Dweblogic.system.BootIdentityFile=
  <Domain home/myboot.txt>
```

After restarting the AdminServer, it had encrypted my password and username in `myboot.txt` file.

In case you want the `boot.properties` file to be removed, the following option can be used:

```
-Dweblogic.system.RemoveBootIdentity=true
```

This can be used even when you have specified a custom `boot.properties` file.

If you have specified both the options:

```
--Dweblogic.system.BootIdentityFile=<Domain home/myboot.txt>
- Dweblogic.system.RemoveBootIdentity=true
```

then after a start of Admin Server, `myboot.txt` will be deleted — just in case you are not sure what is Admin Server username and password.

Server states and transitions

Every time you try to manipulate a WebLogic server, it ends up in some kind of state after your action. These states can be:

- STANDBY
- STARTING
- ADMIN
- RESUMING
- RUNNING

An overview of Server states and transitions

In the following diagram you see the several server instance states:

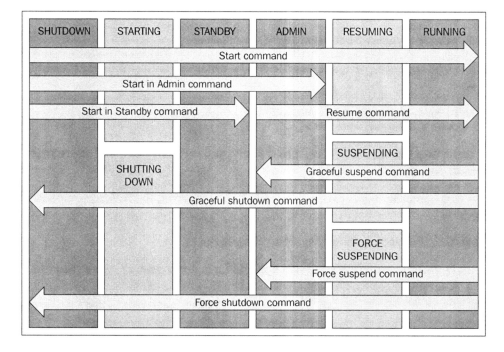

Stopping the WebLogic Server

There are some different shutdown options available to stop WebLogic Server:

Graceful:

Stop the server from the Administration Console, on the **Control** Tab in the Servers Health section.

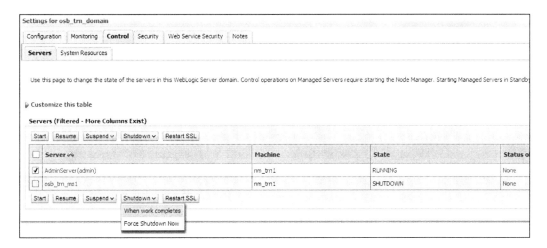

This also closes the Administration Console, so restarting requires a command-line action.

Abrupt:

Press *Ctrl + C* to interrupt the startWebLogic program when using it in the foreground (so, without `nohup`) or kill it to filterout the process number with `ps -ef | grep <PID>`, and then kill it.

Usually, your applications are running on Managed Servers, not on the Administration Server; so even though this is abrupt, it is not disruptive.

Another way to stop is to use the `stopWeblogic.sh` script, which you can find in the Domain home, under `/bin`. For Managed Server instances, you should use `stopManagedWebLogic.sh`.

Another way to stop your WebLogic domain is to use WLST and the node manager. This will be discussed in *Chapter 13, WLST: Makes an Administrator's Life Easier.*

Ease of use: The Administration Console

One of the most important items for an administrator is the Administration Console (or here) Administration Console. It's the central point where all tasks come together, such as:

- Monitoring
- Control
- Configuration
- Security
- Deployment of applications
- Diagnostics and logging

The Administration Console can be accessed after startup at `http://<weblogicserver><port>/console`. The login screen appears. Enter the WebLogic credentials and you're in! The following screenshot is an example of the same:

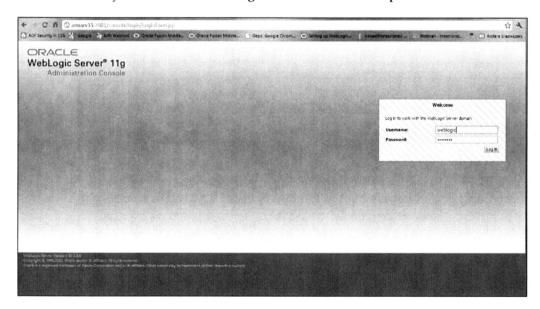

Components of the Administration Console

After you have logged in, the following screen appears in your browser.

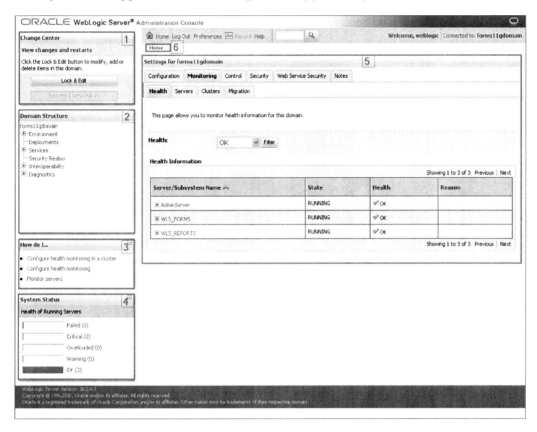

- Change Center
- Domain Structure
- Help Center
- System Status
- Work area
- Breadcrumbs

The Change Center

When you run WebLogic Server in Production Mode, the Change Center will be active. This keeps track of who does what and locks when an Administrator performs a session. The console gets locked for that user and can only be changed unless the session has been activated or released. This mechanism prevents other users logging in to the console and doing configuration changes before you are finished.

First you must click on the **Lock & Edit** Button, and then you can do the necessary work. When it's completed, you click on **Activate Changes**.

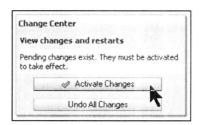

Now, click on the **View changes and restarts** link on the second tab, to see what items should be restarted.

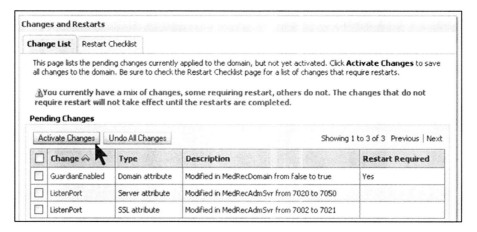

The Domain Structure

Also on the left, you can find a navigation tree called the **Domain Structure**. In here, you can access all configurable resources within the WebLogic Server, such as:

- Server: such as Administration Server, Managed Servers, and Clusters
- Services: such as JDBC and JMS
- Deployments: Applications, Adapters, and Libraries
- Security: Providers, Encryption keys, and wallets
- Diagnostics and Logging.

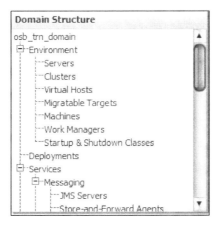

The System Status

The **System Status** panel reports on the number of information, error, and warning messages that have been logged. You can view these messages in the server log files, which you can access from the Administration Console at **Diagnostics | Log Files**.

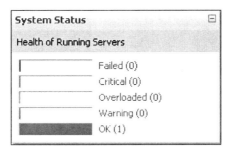

Breadcrumbs

In the taskbar, you can track your previous navigation using the Breadcrumbs, so you can jump back two or three steps before.

Home >Summary of Servers >**AdminServer**

Disabling and enabling the Administration Console

For companies, such as FinanceFiction, which have strict security, administrators are only allowed to use the console if needed. Otherwise it should be set to off. Here's how to disable or enable it.

To disable:

1. Select your domain name in the Domain Structure panel of the console.

2. Select **Configuration | General**, and click **Advanced** at the bottom of the page, and untick Console Enabled.

3. To enable, you can use WLST. The following code shows how to do it:

```
connect("username","password")
edit()
startEdit()
cmo.setConsoleEnabled(true)
save()
activate()
The following attribute(s) have been changed on MBeans which
require server re-start.
MBean Changed : com.bea:Name=mydomain,Type=Domain Attributes
changed :
ConsoleEnabled
Activation completed
disconnect()
exit()
```

Set the Administration Port

An administrator can separate the WebLogic Admin Server port from its administration tasks. For this you can enable the Administration Port.

With the Administration Port enabled:

1. The console is only accessible over a non-standard port (which should not be available from outside your firewall). You have to use SSL.

2. You get a dedicated administration listen thread.

3. Administrative requests over any port other than the Admin Port are rejected.

So, by using the Admin Port, you protect your console and get several other benefits. The Admin Port will not be on port 80 or 443 and will thus not be available outside your firewall. Technically, you could open the Admin Port on the firewall but then you're back in the same boat. Also, anybody who tries to do an administrative request over any other port will find their request rejected.

Another feature is that your interaction with the console has to be over SSL, which protects your data as it transits the wire.

Guarding your WebLogic Server: Protect against overload

When you install WebLogic Server out of the box, the configuration shipped with it is pretty standard. As an administrator, you should be a guardian of the overall performance. Sure, there are many causes which can drill down performance, availability or whatever, but here are some general steps to start with. Following these rules may save you a whole lot of work afterwards.

Limiting requests by throttling the thread pool

In WebLogic Server, all requests, whether related to system administration or application activity, are serviced through a single thread pool. To avoid managing overloaded requests, you can throttle the thread pool by defining a maximum queue length. If the configured value has been reached, WebLogic Server will refuse requests, except for requests on the administration channel. In this setup, WebLogic Server will not run out of resources. Think of hackers who will bombard many requests at a time in order to overload your system. Limiting it will block any other access up to the value you have set.

Set the Shared Capacity for Work Managers field in the Administration Console (see **Environments | Servers | server_name | Configuration | Overload**).

Limiting HTTP sessions

You should limit the number of active HTTP sessions based on detection of a low memory condition. This is useful to avoid out of memory exceptions. WebLogic Server refuses requests that create new HTTP sessions after the configured threshold has been reached. In a WebLogic Server cluster, the proxy plug-in redirects a refused request to another Managed Server in the cluster. A nonclustered server instance can redirect requests to alternative server instances.The Servlet container takes one of the following actions when the maximum number of sessions is reached. If the server instance is in a cluster, the Servlet container throws a `SessionCreationException`.

Your application code should handle this runtime exception and send a relevant response. To implement overload protection, you should handle this exception and send a 503 response explicitly. This response can then be handled by the proxy or load balancer.

You set a limit for the number of simultaneous HTTP sessions in the deployment descriptor for the Web application. For example, the following element sets a limit of 12 sessions:

```
<session-descriptor>
<max-in-memory-sessions>12</max-in-memory-sessions>
</session-descriptor>
```

"Out of Memory" exceptions

To improve application stability, you could implement a system exit when an "Out of Memory" occurs in a certain Managed Server instance. This can be done to add this in the domain `config.xml` (located in `<domain_home/config>`).

```
<overload-protection>
  <panic-action>system-exit</panic-action>
</overload-protection>
```

To overcome unavailability — in this case (when the Managed Server stops working!) you should implement crash recovery with the Node Manager (will be discussed in *Chapter 5, Managed Servers and the Node Manager*).

Stuck thread handling

First, what is a stuck thread? WebLogic uses threads to do its tasks. When certain tasks can't be done, because it is waiting for an answer (such as waiting for an answer from a remote database), then at a certain time it stops asking and will be flagged as a stuck thread.

WebLogic Server checks for stuck threads periodically. If all application threads are stuck, a server instance marks itself failed, and if configured to do so, exits change into the Server Instance terminates its work. You can configure Node Manager to restart for automatic failure recovery.

You can configure these actions to occur when not all threads are stuck, but the numbers of stuck threads have exceeded a configured threshold:

1. Shut down the Work Manager if it has stuck threads. A Work Manager that is shutdown will refuse new work and reject existing work in the queue by sending a rejection message. In a cluster, clustered clients will fail over to another cluster member.

2. Shut down the application if there are stuck threads in the application. The application is shutdown changing it into ADMIN mode. All work managers belonging to the application are shut down, and behave as described earlier.

The following is an example of an application with problems:

```
"ExecuteThread: '52' for queue: 'default'" daemon prio=5
tid=0x4b3e40b0
  nid=0x1170 waiting on monitor [0x4c74f000..0x4c74fdbc]
  at java.lang.Object.wait(Native Method)
  at WebLogic.rjvm.ResponseImpl.waitForData(ResponseImpl.java:72)
  at WebLogic.rjvm.ResponseImpl.getTxContext(ResponseImpl.java:97)
  at WebLogic.rmi.internal.BasicOutboundRequest.sendReceive(
BasicOutboundRequest.java:80)
  at WebLogic.rmi.cluster.ReplicaAwareRemoteRef.invoke(
ReplicaAwareRemoteRef.java:262)
  at WebLogic.rmi.cluster.ReplicaAwareRemoteRef.invoke(
ReplicaAwareRemoteRef.java:229)
  at WebLogic.rmi.internal.ProxyStub.invoke(ProxyStub.java:35)
  at $Proxy6.lookup(Unknown Source)
  at WebLogic.jndi.internal.WLContextImpl.lookup(WLContextImpl.
java:341)
```

Overview of the available System Administrator tools

To be a proper administrator, you need some tools. There are many tools available, but let's sum up the most important ones:

- Administration Console
- WebLogic Scripting Tool
- config.sh/bat
- Configuration Template Builder
- Apache Ant tasks
- SNMP agents

Administration Console

The Administration Console is a Web application hosted by the WebLogic Admin Server. Through the Administration Console, system administrators can easily perform all WebLogic Server management tasks without having to learn the JMX API or the underlying management architecture. The Administration Server keeps changes to attributes in the `config.xml` file for the domain you are managing.

WebLogic Scripting Tool

The WebLogic Scripting Tool (WLST) is a command-line scripting interface that you use to manage and monitor active or inactive WebLogic Server domains. The WLST scripting environment is based on the Java scripting interpreter Jython.

WLST will be discussed in *Chapter 13*, *WLST: Makes an Administrator's Life Easier*.

Configuration Wizard

The Configuration Wizard creates the appropriate directory structure for a WebLogic Server domain, the config.xml file, and scripts you can use to start the servers in your domain. The wizard uses templates to create domains, and you can customize these templates to duplicate your own domains.

You can also use the Configuration Wizard to add or remove services from an existing, inactive domain. It can be executed with a script, config.sh or config.cmd (Windows).

Apache Ant tasks

You can use two Ant tasks shipped with WebLogic Server to help you perform common configuration tasks in a development environment. Ant is a Java-based tool. The configuration tasks let you start and stop WebLogic Server instances as well as create and configure WebLogic Server domains.

SNMP

A tool based on the Simple Network Management Protocol (SNMP). WebLogic Server SNMP agents let you integrate management of WebLogic Servers into an SNMP-compliant management system that gives you a single view of the various software and hardware resources of a complex, distributed system.

JMX

A handy API to manage WebLogic subsystems is JMX (JAVA Management Extensions) for monitoring and managing resources. Like other management standards, JMX is a public specification and many vendors of commonly used monitoring products support it.

Some tools are:

- JConsole & JVisualVM– shipped with Sun JDK
- Open Source JMX Browsers
    - jManage, EJTools JMX Browser, MC4J, …

- WLST
    - ° Wraps MBean access for popular operations
    - ° Supports 'basic' JMX access for all MBeans
- From Java
    - ° Java application can use `javax.management` to access MBeans in remote MBean servers
- FMW Enterprise Manager System MBean Browser

MBeans—the heart of the JMX specification

MBeans are configurable JAVA Objects in WebLogic, which can be accessed to change, configure, or control your WebLogic environment.

There are three types of MBeans:

1. Administration (domain wide)
2. Configuration (local on Managed Server)
3. Runtime (local on Managed Server)

The MBeans are organized in a tree, starting at the domain root (DomainMBean).

Every WLS object (domain, server) and JEE resource (JDBC DS, JMS Queue) is represented by an MBean.

Deployment API

A built-in tool within WebLogic Server is the Deployment API, to deploy applications, adapters, and libraries. Deployment will be discussed in *Chapter 6, Deploy your Applications in Oracle WebLogic.*

Logging API

To detect and analyze problems, logging is very important. WebLogic provides many ways of logging; this will be discussed in *Chapter 11, Configuring and Analyzing Logging.*

WLDF

WLDF, WebLogic Diagnostics Framework, is a group of components that work together to collect, archive, and access diagnostic information. It gathers diagnostics in real-time.

This will also be discussed in *Chapter 11, Configuring and Analyzing Logging.*

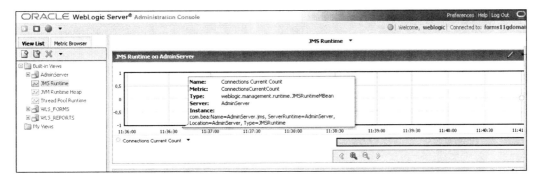

Summary

So, this was a heavy chapter, wasn't it? Well, an administrator's life gets easier the more knowledge you gain. You're now already miles ahead of your colleagues; you're becoming a real expert now!

And you're going to need it, because application development teams are already knocking at your door, wanting to deploy their applications. But, before you start with that, first start with the other important items in WebLogic: The Managed Server and the Node Manager.

5
Managed Servers and the Node Manager

"I've got to manage more resources!", your boss yells one day when the stress is getting too much for him. Lots of work to do and less people, but you know better. With the proper management and dedication of resources, all the work can be done within the required timeframe without any extra resources.

You have already learned a lot about Oracle WebLogic, and you saw how it manages its resources. Let's take a deeper look into two important components of WebLogic: Managed Servers and the Node Manager.

Managed Servers

In a domain, server instances other than the Administration Server are called Managed Servers. Managed Servers host the components and associated resources that constitute your applications. When a Managed Server starts up, it connects to the domain's Administration Server to obtain configuration and deployment settings.

Two or more Managed Servers can be configured as a *WebLogic Server Cluster* to increase application scalability, availability, and load. In a WebLogic Server cluster, most resources and services are deployed identically to each Managed Server (enabling failover and load balancing). A single domain can contain multiple WebLogic Server clusters, as well as multiple Managed Servers that are not configured as clusters. For more information about the benefits and capabilities of a WebLogic Server cluster, see *Chapter 8* , *Making Your WebLogic Mission Critical: Clustering*.

From an O/S perspective, a Managed Server is a running process that consumes an amount of processor time and RAM, specified in the start-parameters. A Managed Server is in fact a Java Virtual Machine (JVM) that uses a certain amount of memory, which is specified in the JVM startup parameters.

A Java Virtual Machine (JVM) runs on top of the machine's O/S in which Java programs can be executed. JVM is a byte code interpreter that reads and executes all Java classes. Each O/S has its own version of a Virtual Machine (Windows, Linux, Solaris, and AIX). JVMs will be discussed further in *Chapter 9, The Heart of Oracle WebLogic: The JVM*.

Managed Servers configuration

You can configure Managed Servers in three ways:

- Domain Configuration Wizard
- Administration Console
- Command Line (WLST)

Domain Configuration Wizard

During domain creation, one of the options you can use is to create one or more Managed Servers. This is optional, so it can be done later as well. In the **Optional Configuration** screen check the **Managed Servers, Clusters and Machines** option to enter the **Managed Server configuration** screen. You can set the following screen to configure your Managed Server(s).

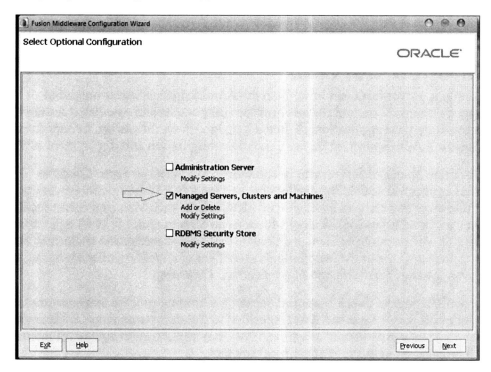

When selected, you will have to fill in:

- A name for your Managed Server.

- A listen address, typically the address the AdminServer is listening on. It depends on the IP address of the machine you want to run this Managed Server on.

- A listen port.

- Optionally, you can specify to use an SSL Listen port and check the **SSL enabled**.

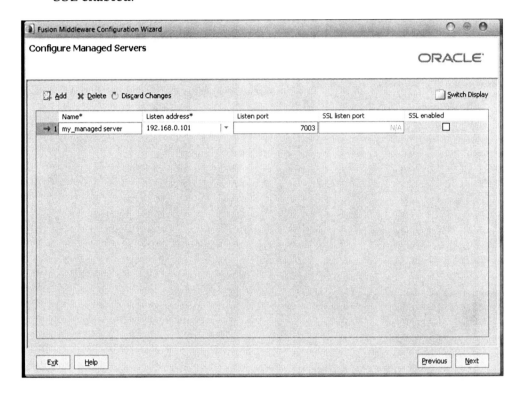

 Set the listen address to an internal IP address or hostname, when you use another network interface for external IP. If you use an internal network for administration tasks, you could use more network interfaces (physical or virtual) to arrange which traffic is coming in on which interface.

When the Managed Servers configuration screen is completed, a few other screens appear, which we will discuss later in this chapter, namely Node Manager and another one, Clustering, which will be discussed in *Chapter 8, Making Your WebLogic Mission Critical: Clustering*.

Finally, you can create or extend the domain with your newly created Managed Server(s).

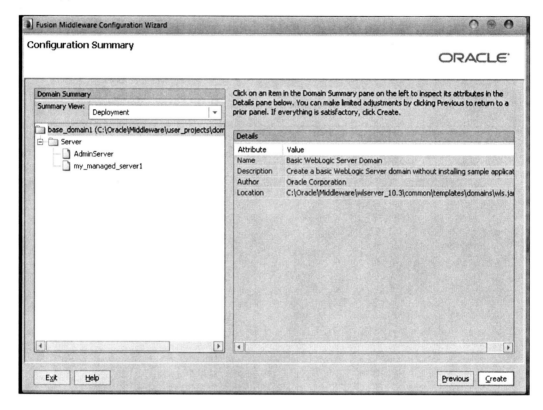

So, that was all! Easy, wasn't it?. Of course here it just begins, but first let's have a look at the other ways of creating Managed Servers.

Creation through the WebLogic Administration Console

Another way of creating a Managed Server is through the WebLogic Administration Console.

1. Navigate to the **Domain Structure | Servers | Configuration** tab.

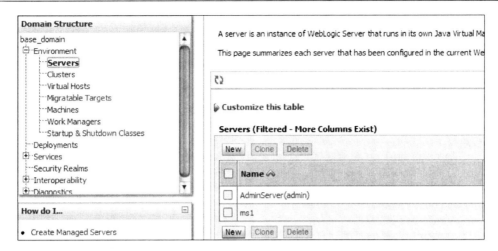

2. Click on **New**, and here you can create a new Managed Server.

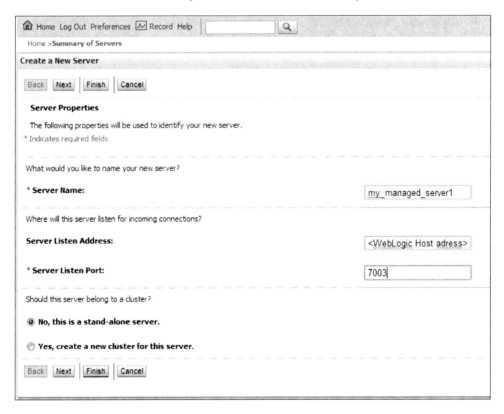

3. In the previous screen, you specify your Managed Server. The **Server Listen Port** should be set to a port that is not already occupied.

Creation with WebLogic Scripting Tool

Of course, this can be done using WebLogic Scripting Tool as well, but when you have to roll out a large number of WebLogic Servers, then it could be very useful to use WLST.

1. Start WLST with the help of the following command:

   ```
   $WL_HOME/common/bin/wlst.sh
   ```

   You will end up in the WLST prompt in the offline mode.

2. When you are in the WLST prompt, enter the following block of code:

   ```
   wls:/offline> connect('weblogic','mypassword','t3://
   localhost:7001')
    Connecting to t3://localhost:7020 with userid weblogic ...
    Successfully connected to Admin Server 'AdminServer'
    that belongs to domain 'base_domain'.
   wls:/Base_domain/serverConfig> cd('Servers')
   wls:/Base_domain/serverConfig/Servers> edit()
   wls:/Base_domain/edit> startEdit()
   wls:/Base_domain/edit !> server1=create('my_managed_
   server1','Server')
    MBean type Server with name my_managed_server1 has been created
   successfully.
   wls:/Base_domain/edit !> server1.getName()
    'my_managed_server1'
   wls:/Base_domain/edit !> ls('Servers')
    drw-    AdminServer
    drw-    my_managed_server1

   wls:/Base_domain/edit !> save()
   wls:/Base_domain/edit !> activate()
   wls:/Base_domain/edit !> stopEdit()
   wls:/Base_domain/edit> exit()
   ```

In the script, you first make a connection with the Administration server. You have to connect to the domain, before you can actually make any changes. The second thing to do is to start an edit session, in which you create this simple Managed Server. After creating it, you issue the getName() on the newly created server to see if your Managed Server has been created. If so, you save and activate your changes. You stop the edit session by issuing stopEdit(); the editing session will be saved and stopped.

After you create a Managed Server, it is not running yet, so let's have a look at the several ways to start and stop them.

Starting Managed Servers

There are several ways to start a Managed Server:

- Using a startup script: `<DOMAIN Home>/bin/startManagedWebLogic.sh`
- `weblogic.Server` command in combination with Java
- WLST and Node Manager
- Administration Console
  - ° Requires Node Manager on each machine and extra configuration such as:
    - Username and password
    - Listen ports
    - Start parameters specified like `CLASSPATH`, `JAVA_PATH`

Start using the startManagedWeblogic script

Start/Stop scripts are provided by default on domain creation. These scripts can be modified if need be.

For starting a Managed Server, there is the `startManagedWeblogic.sh` script.

To start, execute the following command:

```
startManagedWeblogic.sh <managed_server_name> admin_url:admin_port
```

This is starting in a foreground process, and if you click *Ctrl +C* it will be stopped.

```
<Feb 2, 2011 12:01:32 PM EST> <Notice> <WebLogicServer> <BEA-000330> <Started WebLogic Managed Server
    "My_Managed_Server1" for domain "MyDomain" running in Production Mode>
<Feb 2, 2011 12:01:36 PM EST> <Notice> <Cluster> <BEA-000102> <Joining cluster MedRecClust1 on
    192.168.0.1:7009>
<Feb 2, 2011 12:01:36 PM EST> <Notice> <WebLogicServer> <BEA-000365> <Server state changed to RUNNING>
<Feb 2, 2011 12:01:36 PM EST> <Notice> <WebLogicServer> <BEA-000360> <Server started in RUNNING mode>
```

WLST and the Node Manager

However, the Node Manager will be discussed later in this chapter. One of the ways to start a Managed Server in combination with the Node Manager is as follows:

1. First, start a WLST session by running the `wlst.sh` or `wlst.cmd` (located in the WL Server home).

2. Then you start the node:

   ```
   startNodeManager(verbose='true',
   NodeManagerHome=<WL_SERVER>/common/nodemanager',
   ListenPort='5556')
   ```

3. Then, you will have to connect with the Node Manager and stop or start your Managed Server:

```
nmConnect('weblogic', 'weblogic', 'localhost', '5556','mydomain',
'<WL_DOMAIN_DIR'>)
wls:/nm/mydomain>nmStart('serverName')
```

4. To stop, use the following code:

```
wls:/nm/mydomain>nmKill('serverName')
```

Start with the Admin Console

When you configure the Node Manager properly, Managed Servers can be started and stopped with the Admin Console.

Navigate to the **System Health** section and click the **Control** tab, here you can stop and start your servers.

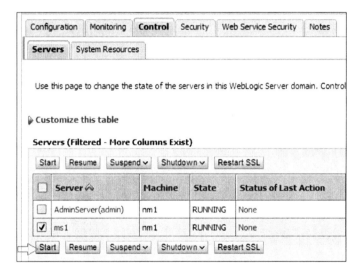

Running modes of a Managed Server

A Managed Server gets its configuration during startup (and when changes occur) from the Admin Server and stores it in its local `config` subdirectory.

By default, Managed Servers can function independently of the Administration Server. This is called the Managed Server Independent mode or MSI mode. A Managed Server instance can start in MSI mode even when the Administration Server is unavailable. But without a running Administration Server, the Managed Servers won't receive any configuration changes.

To start a Managed Server in MSI mode:

1. Ensure that the Managed Server's root directory contains the `config` subdirectory.

2. If the `config` subdirectory does not exist, copy it from the Administration Server's root directory.

3. Start the Managed Server at the command line or by using a script.

Start as a Windows service

For Windows systems, you can create a service to manipulate the start and stop of the WebLogic Admin Server and/or the Managed Servers so that they run as a background process. In this way, you can also configure them to start automatically when the server reboots.

The steps to be taken are as follows:

Create a script

The script that you create must set values for variables that identify the name of the server instance and other server-specific information. It must then call a master script, such as `WL Server Home\server\bin\installSvc.cmd`. The master script invokes the *beasvc* utility, which adds a key to the Windows Registry.

The script should contain the following parameters:

- `SETLOCAL`

  Localization of environment variables in a batch file.

- Set `DOMAIN_NAME`=domain-name

  Here, domain name is the name of your WebLogic Server domain.

- Set `USERDOMAIN_HOME`=path_to your_domain

- Set `SERVER_NAME`=server-name

  Here, server-name is the name of an existing server instance that you want to set up as a Windows service.

- Set `WLS_USER`=username

- Set `WLS_PW`=password

  The *beasvc* utility encrypts the login credentials and stores them in the Windows registry.

- Set `PRODUCTION_MODE`=true

- Set `JAVA_OPTIONS`=java-options

Here, java-options are one or more Java arguments that you want to pass to the Java Virtual Machine (JVM). They are separate, multiple arguments with a space.

- Set `JAVA_VM`=-JVM-mode

Such as, `-client` or `-server`.

- Set `MEM_ARGS`=[-Xms…] [-Xmx…]

    This can be used for the sizing of your JVM. For more information, see *Chapter 9, The Heart of Oracle WebLogic: The JVM*.

There are some more options, but these are the most important ones. Also add the following line and then run the script:

```
call "WL_HOME\server\bin\installSvc.cmd"
ENDLOCAL
```

Save it as a `*`.cmd file, and run it. After this, the service should appear in your Services list.

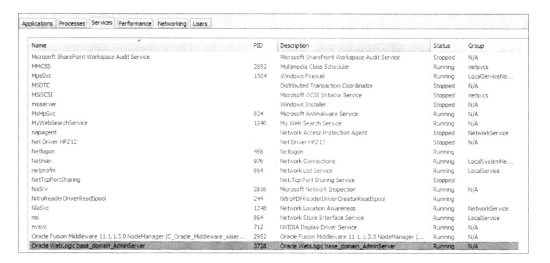

The WebLogic Server Lifecycle

Every time you change a certain state of one of your servers (Admin or Managed) the Lifecycle state will be updated to a new level.

There are several kinds of states, namely:

- **SHUTDOWN**: The server is configured but inactive.

- **STARTING**: This is a transition state. The server cannot accept any client or administrative requests as it is obtaining its configuration data. A lot of services are started during this state, such as the `weblogic.t3.srvr.BootService`, which includes basic services, such as kernel and execute queues.

- **ADMIN**: In the ADMIN state, WebLogic Server is up and running, but available only for administration operations, and it allows you to perform server and application-level administration tasks. In this state, the Admin console is accessible only to admin users, applications, and resources that are also in the ADMIN state. Also when a subsystem fails on startup, WebLogic can go into ADMIN state.

- **RESUMING**: In this state, the server ends up its starting sequences and is getting prepared for the RUNNING state.

- **RUNNING**: In this state, the server is fully functional.

- **SUSPENDING**: In this state, it performs the operations required to place itself in the ADMIN state, suspending a subset of subsystems and services in an ordered fashion, and completing.

- **FORCE_SUSPENDING**: In this state, the server is forcibly setting itself into the ADMIN state.

- **SHUTTING DOWN**: A normal controlled shutdown state.

- **FAILED**: This is a state you don't like to see, but of course it can occur. If it failed before reaching the ADMIN state, the server instance shuts itself down.

These states can be verified in the console, the server logs, and through WLST.

The Node Manager

In the previous pages, you might have noticed that the Node Manager is being used for several tasks. So, what is the Node Manager and how is it being used?

You can use Node Managers to:

- Start, shut down, and restart an Administration Server

- Start, shut down, suspend, and restart Managed Servers

- Automatically restart the Administration and Managed Servers on failure

- Monitor servers and collect log data

Node Managers:

- Run on the same computers as the Managed Servers
- Can be run automatically in the background, as Windows services or UNIX daemons
- Are available as either Java-based, or script-based processes (for UNIX only)

In fact, the Node Manager is an O/S running process which acts like a watchdog over your WebLogic Server; the Node Manager is nothing more than an operating system process running in a JVM.

The idea is that the Node Manager process is not associated with a specific WebLogic domain but with a machine. You can use the same Node Manager process to control WebLogic Server instances in any WebLogic Server domain, as long as the server these instances reside on is the same machine as the Node Manager process. The Node Manager process must run on each server that hosts WebLogic server instances — Administration or Managed Server — that you want to control with Node Manager.

Some important things to know:

- Configurations are stored under the `<WL Server Home>/common/ nodemanager` in the `nodemanager.properties`
- The domains controlled by the Node Manager are stored in the `nodemanager.domains file` in that same directory
- Domain-specific configurations are stored in the domain directory under `servers/<name of server>/ startup.properties`

Within Windows, Node Manager can run as a service. Under Linux/UNIX, there's no out-of-the-box daemon configuration available, so you will have to create that yourself. For this, there is an installation script available, which is `installNodeManagerSvccmd`.

Versions of Node Manager

There are 2 versions of the Node Manager:

- Script based
- Java based

Script-based Node Manager

Typically for *NIX-like systems, WebLogic provides a Node Manager script to start the Node Manager. This is less secure than the Java-based version. However, the advantage of the script-based Node Manager is that it can remotely manage servers over a network that has been configured to use SSH. No additional server installation is required.

Configuring a script-based Node Manager

The SSH Node Manager is a shell script, `wlscontrol.sh`, located in `WL_HOME/common/bin/`. The file must exist on each machine that hosts server instances that you want to control with Node Manager. You must also have a SSH client executable on each.

You must create a SSH public key on each machine on which you want to use the script-based version because you want to start the script remotely without having to fill in credentials.

After you've configured remote SSH and your WebLogic clustered domain, you can start the AdminServer with:

```
WL_HOME/common/bin/wlscontrol.sh -d clustdomain -r
DOMAIN_HOME -c -f startWebLogic.sh -s AdminServer START
```

Each machine that will host a Managed Server will have a duplicate domain created and configured.

From a local terminal, create a new empty directory in the home directory for the O/S user, on each of the Managed Server host machines and also on a back-up machine.

As the O/S user, use WLST to enroll the user's home directory as being the base directory to remotely run servers.

For example:

```
WL_HOME/common/bin/wlst.sh
connect('weblogic','weblogic','t3://,WL_SERVER>:7001')
nmEnroll('/home/<O/S user>/clustdomain','/home//<O/S user>/')
exit()
```

Be sure to run `nmEnroll` on each remote machine. This command creates a property file, `/home/<O/S user>/nodemanager.domains`, which maps domain names to home directories, and creates the required domain configuration and security information, so that Managed Servers can communicate with the Administration server.

The `nodemanager.domains` file removes the need to specify the domain home directory (with `-r`) when starting `wlscontrol.sh`. However, since you changed the Node Manager home directory, you must specify `-n /home/ndmgr`. The default Node Manager home directory is `WL_HOME//common/nodemanager.domains`; you might not want to use this directory as it is in the product installation directory and owned by another useTry to start your Managed Servers.

Local:

```
WL_HOME/common/bin/wlscontrol.sh -d clustdomain -n
/home/<OSUser> c -f startManagedWebLogic.sh -s MS1 START
```

Remote:

```
ssh -l OSuser -o PasswordAuthentication=no -p 22 <ipadress>
<WL_HOME>/common/bin/wlscontrol.sh -d clustdomain -n /
home/OSUser -c -f startManagedWebLogic.sh -s MS1 START
```

Java-based Node Manager

The Java-based Node Manager runs as an O/S Java Virtual Machine process. On Windows, you can install it as a service using the `installNodeMgrSvc.cmd`. You should configure the port and listen address in this script.

An important configuration file is the `nodemanager.properties`, located in the `<WL_HOME>/common/nodemanager`.

An important thing to do is to set the properties `StartScriptEnabled` and `StopScriptEnabled` to `true`. When the Node Manager starts on a WebLogic Server, it will now use the `startWebLogic` script. This script calls the `setDomainEnv.sh` (`setWLEnv.sh`) script, which sets the server's classpath.

If you leave this to `false`, starting the WebLogic Server instance might not be successful as key components fail to start because of classpath errors.

Another interesting parameter you might want to set is `CrashRecoveryEnabled`. You can set this to true when you want a Managed Server to be restarted when it has crashed. Because configuring a Node Manager can be quite confusing for new WebLogic administrators, I'll explain this in a few easy steps.

1. Create a Machine in the AdminConsole or during domain creation, and attach your servers to it.

 Use a UNIX Machine for `*NIX` systems, "Other" for Windows.

2. Startup the Node Manager in the foreground:

   `<WL_HOME>/server/bin/startNodemanager.sh`

   The property file and domains file will be created in:

   `<WL_HOME>/common/nodemanager.`

3. Edit the `nodemanager.properties` for your needs, such as `StartScriptEnabled` and `StopScriptEnabled`, `CrashRecoveryEnabled`, and `ListenAddress`.

Configuring a Java-based Node Manager as an xinetd service

Just as a Windows Service, on `*NIX` systems you can configure the Node Manager to run as an inetd or xinetd service.

Ensure that NodeManagerHome and other system properties are defined, such as CLASSPATH, LD Library Path, Java Options, and Node Manager Options.

If xinetd is configured with `libwrap`, you should add the `NOLIBWRAP` flag. Ensure that the `hosts.deny` and `hosts.allow` files are configured correctly. Please ask your O/S administrator. Depending on your network environment, additional configuration may be necessary.

The following example shows how Node Manager can be configured within xinetd:

```
# default: off
# description:nodemanager as a service
service nodemgrsvc
{
   type            = UNLISTED
   disable         = no
```

```
socket_type     = stream
protocol        = tcp
wait            = yes
user            = <username>
port            = 5556
flags           = NOLIBWRAP
log_on_success  = DURATION HOST USERID
server          = <path-to-java>/java
env             = CLASSPATH=<cp> LD_LIBRARY_PATH=<ldpath>
server_args     = -client -DNodeManagerHome=<NMHome> <java
options>
    <nodemanager options> weblogic.NodeManager -v
```

As root just run the following:

```
root@app1 xinetd.d]# service xinetd restart
Stopping xinetd: [ OK ]
Starting xinetd: [ OK ]
[rootapp1 xinetd.d]# /
```

Then, always make sure it is running:

```
[[root@app1 xinetd.d]# service xinetd status
xinetd (pid 1699) is running...
[root@app1 xinetd.d]# netstat -nap|grep 5556
tcp 0 0 0.0.0.0:5556 0.0.0.0:* LISTEN 1699/xinetd
[root@app1 xinetd.d]$ ps -ef|grep java
weblogic 3081 3076 2 18:29 ? 00:00:04 java -client -DNodeManagerHome=/
u01/app/oracle/product/middleware/wlserver_10.3/common/nodemanager
-Xverify:none

-Djava.security.policy=/usr/app/oracle/product/middleware/wlserver_10.3/
server/lib/weblogic.policy

-Dweblogic.nodemanager.javaHome=/usr/app/oracle/product/
  middleware/Jrockit weblogic.NodeManager -v
```

Because the configuring of a Node Manager can be quite a confusing issue for new WebLogic administrators, I'll explain this in a few easy steps:

On `*NIX`:

1. Create a Machine in the AdminConsole or during domain creation, and attach your servers to it.

 Use a UNIX Machine for `*NIX` systems, "Other" for Windows.

2. Start up the Node Manager in the foreground:

   `<WL Server HOME>/server/bin/startNodemanager.sh`

   The property file and domains file will be created in `<WL Server HOME>/common/nodemanager`. Edit the `nodemanager.properties` for your needs, such as `StartScriptEnabled` and `StopScriptEnabled`, `CrashRecoveryEnabled`, and `ListenAddress`.

3. Now start the Node Manager in the background:

   `nohup <WL_HOME>/server/bin/startNodemanager.sh  &`

Running a Node Manager as a Windows service

Although during installation the Node Manager will be created as a service, here's how to do it manually.

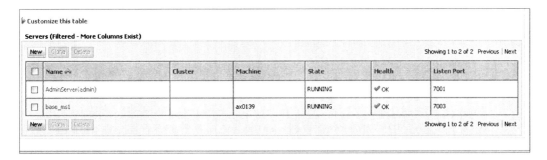

1. Configure the Node Manager Properties File.

   Go to `WL_HOME/common/nodemanager` and open `nodemanager.properties`. Change the following properties to:

   ```
   CrashRecoveryEnabled=true
   StartScriptEnabled=true
   ```

2. Install Node Manager as a Windows Service.

3. Execute the following script:

`WL_HOME/server/bin/installNodeMgrSvc.cmd.`

This should create a Windows Service called *Oracle WebLogic Node Manager (PATH_TO_DOMAIN)*. Go to **Windows Services** and double-click on it. On the **Log On** tab, check the option **This Account** and provide the user/ password you plan to use to run the WebLogic Server under Windows. Click on **OK** and start the service.

4. Start the AdminServer.

Open a command prompt at `MW_HOME/user_projects/DOMAIN_NAME/bin` and run the following script `setDomainEnv.cmd`. In the same command prompt window, type: `startWebLogic.cmd`. The AdminServer should start now.

5. Start the Managed Servers.

Open a browser and go to `http://HOST:PORT/console`. On the **Domain Structure** panel (upper left), click on **Servers**. On the **Summary of Servers** (middle right), go to the **Control** tab and select **ms1** and **ms2** and then click on **Start**. The ms1 and ms2 should start now.

6. Test the work.

    Let's go to the Windows Task Manager and check if our servers are there running. Open the Task Manager (right-click on the Windows clock and select the **Task Manager** option from the contextual menu) and sort the column **Image Name**. Now, let's look for our Java processes.

In the previous screenshot, you can see Java processes, one for *AdminServer*, one for *ms1* and *ms2* respectively. You can also find the Node Manager process, it's something similar to `beasvc.exe`. Now, let's simulate a server crash, let's kill our servers processes. Select the Java processes and click on the **End Process** button. In this way, the server is abruptly shut down and to the Node Manager this means a server crash. The Node Manager will then restart the processes, and they will appear again on the Task Manager just a few seconds after you've killed it. To simulate a complete OS crash, let's kill the Node Manager process first (`beasvc.exe`) and then kill the Java processes. Now, the Java processes won't come back because the Node Manager is not running. After rebooting Windows, we can see that the Node Manager starts automatically, and just after that the Java processes begin to show up on the Task Manager.

Summary

Well, you're again a step closer to being in control of your WebLogic Server environments.

This weekend you received a phone call, and your nervous boss was yelling on the other side of the line, "There has been a power outage!! Rush to the office and start WebLogic!!"

You laughed, and said to him while staying really calm, "Don't worry… the Node Manager will keep them in control…"

A few minutes later your boss, after verifying it, stumbles and says, "They…they are already up! You're worth a million!"

Well, at least until the next challenge you are about to face, in the next chapter!

6
Deploy Your Applications in Oracle WebLogic

In the previous chapters of this book, you were introduced to the world of middleware, JEE, application servers, and of course in particular the Oracle WebLogic Server. You have learned how to install the WebLogic Server software, how to configure, and set up your WebLogic Server.

Meanwhile, when you were busy installing and configuring your WebLogic Server environment, people of the development department were already busy developing their first applications. Before FinanceFiction decided to use Oracle WebLogic as the strategic platform, all applications were built externally by software vendors. But FinanceFiction invested a lot in recruiting new people, and after getting the right people in, a development team started building new applications. These new applications introduced a lot of new functionalities. They got involved in the project at the same time as your department. One of your installed Oracle WebLogic server environments got a staging environment for developing new applications. These applications would be widely used by many departments in your company.

This morning you received a phone call from the lead developer, and he informed you that the first application was ready for the test phase and that you could start deploying it. Until this moment they used to deploy their applications through their own application development tool, but that would not be the strategy for doing deployments in your final production environment.

First of all, you have to ask yourself this question: what does the term deployment mean?

Deployment

Originally the term "deployment" originated from the military world, where it means "to position troops in readiness for combat".

In fact, we do the same when we perform an application deployment. We position all components of the deployment package, in order to make them ready to perform the tasks meant for them. The only difference is that our deployment won't fight against any enemy, but will help us in getting our information in a fast, reliable, and easy way.

The term *application deployment* refers to the process of making an application, library, or module available for processing client requests in a WebLogic Server domain. This process is actually unpacking the application package components, putting them into directories, and preparing them to work via WebLogic Server and resources.

WebLogic uses the JEE standards of deployment. A standard API is used by deployment tools and application server providers to configure and deploy applications to an application server.

WebLogic Server implements both the JSR-88 Service Provider Interface (SPI) plug-in and model plug-in, to comply with the J2EE 1.4 deployment specification. You can use a basic J2EE 1.4 deployment API deployment tool with the WebLogic Server plug-ins (without using WebLogic Server extensions to the API) to configure, deploy, and redeploy J2EE applications and modules to WebLogic Server (from WebLogic deployment guide).

The *WebLogicDeploymentManager* object is an interface for the WebLogic Server deployment framework.

Deployment components and terminology

Before we dive deeper into the deployment process let's introduce the following terms:

- **Applications**: The definition of an application is not that simple. An application for an end user can be a whole chain of components from user-interface to database, although the user is not aware of all these components. So an application consists of a program or group of programs designed for end users. Application software can be divided into two general classes: systems software and applications software. Systems software consists of low-level programs that interact with the computer at a very basic level.

- **Application module**: It is an XML document that configures JEE resources such as JDBC, JMS, and EJBs. Application modules can be deployed as standalone modules in which their resources are bound to the global JNDI tree (definition of JNDI, see *Chapter 1, Oracle WebLogic: Your First Step into a Middleware World! - Java Naming and Directory Interface*).

- **Application install directory**: It is a WebLogic Server directory structure, designed to help organize deployment files, and generate deployment configuration artifacts for an application or module. Also referred to as an *application root directory*.

- **Application version**: A string value that identifies the version of a deployed application. It is located in the manifest file.

- **Deployment configuration**: The process of defining the deployment descriptor values required to deploy an application to a particular WebLogic Server domain.

- **Deployment descriptor**: It is an XML document used to define the J2EE behavior or WebLogic Server configuration of an application or module at deployment time.

- **Deployment plan**: It is an XML document that defines an application's WebLogic Server deployment configuration for a specific WebLogic Server environment. A deployment plan resides outside the application's archive file, and can apply changes to deployment properties stored in the application's existing WebLogic Server deployment descriptors.

- **Distribution**: It is the process by which WebLogic Server copies deployment source files to target servers for deployment.

- **Production redeployment**: It is the WebLogic Server redeployment strategy that deploys a new version of a production application alongside an older version, while automatically managing HTTP connections to ensure uninterrupted client access.

- **Staging mode**: It is the method WebLogic server uses to make deployment files available to target servers in a domain. Staging modes determine whether files are distributed to target WebLogic Managed Servers before deployment, or not.

The deployment standard: JSR-88

Because JEE implements standards, the deployment should also follow these standards. JSR-88 is a standardization to define standard application programming interfaces (APIs) to enable deployment of JEE applications and standalone modules to JEE platforms.

The following diagram shows the components of a JSR-88-compliant deployment API (Application Programming Interface).

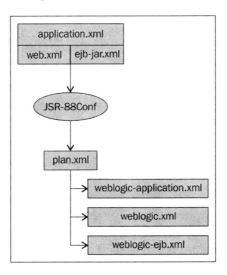

All these following XMLs are standard JEE descriptor files:

- `application.xml`: This is the global application configuration file, which contains the common settings for all application modules contained in the EAR (Enterprise Archive).

- `ejb-jar.xml`: This is the deployment descriptor when deploying an EJB application.

- `web.xml`: This represents the core of a generic Java web application. It provides configuration and deployment information for the Web components that comprise a Web application contained in a WAR (Web Application Archive).

- `weblogic.xml`: This is the WebLogic-specific deployment descriptor file. The `weblogic.xml` deployment descriptor follows a WebLogic-specific schema that is used only by Oracle WebLogic Server. It allows you to enable and configure Web application features that are not part of the JEE specification, such as changing the default root URL path of the Web application or directing application log messages to a dedicated log file.

- `weblogic-application.xml`: This is the WebLogic server-specific deployment descriptor extension for the `application.xml`. Like all the other `weblogic-application.xml` `weblogic-application.xml` WebLogic-specific descriptor files, this file also enables the use of specific WebLogic features that are not a part of the JEE standards.

- `weblogic-ejb-jar.xml`: This is the WebLogic-specific descriptor for deploying an EJB application The `weblogic-ejb-jar.xml` deployment descriptor follows a schema that is used only by Oracle WebLogic Server. It allows you to enable and configure EJB features that are not part of the JEE specification, such as clustering, load balancing, and failover for remote EJBs, tuning EJB performance using pool and cache settings, and many more.

- `plan.xml`: This is an optional XML file associated with an application; it resides outside an application archive and sets or overrides the values in the JEE deployment descriptors. It allows a single application to be easily customized to multiple deployment environments.

Different types of deployment

There are two types of deployment that you can determine:

Archive type

An archive file is a single file that contains all of an application's or module's classes, static files, directories, and deployment descriptor files. In most production environments, the applications that an Administrator receives for deployment are stored as archive files.

Deployment units that are packaged using a jar utility have a specific file extension depending on the type:

- EJBs and client archives are packaged as `.jar` files.

- Web applications are packaged as `.war` files.

- Resource adapters are packaged as `.rar` files.

- Enterprise applications are packaged as `.ear` files, and can contain other Java EE modules, such as EJBs, JDBC, JMS, Web applications, and Resource Adapters.

- Web Services can be packaged either as `.war` files or as `.jar` files, depending on whether they are implemented using Java classes or EJBs. Typically, the `.war` or `.jar` files are then packaged in an `.ear` file.

- Java EE libraries are packaged either as an `.ear` file or as a standard Java EE module.

- Client applications and optional packages are packaged as `.jar` files.

In addition to an archive file, you may also receive a deployment plan, which is a separate file that configures the application for a specific environment.

Exploded type

An exploded type is in fact a non-packaged deployment type. It's a set of directories that contain all the files of the application to be deployed. The directory structure for an exploded archive is very important.

An exploded archive directory contains the same files and directories as a JAR archive. If you choose to use an exploded archive directory, you may be required to manually unpack a previously archived deployment. However, the files and directories reside directly in your filesystem and are not packaged into a single archive file with the jar utility.

To choose for an exploded archive directory could be an option, if you want to perform partial updates of an application after deployment, or if an application contains static files that you will periodically update.

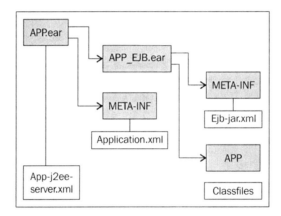

Deployment tools for WebLogic

You can deploy your applications or libraries in several ways, WebLogic provides you several tools for this:

- weblogic.Deployer
- Admin Console and Enterprise Manager Console
- WLST
- wldeploy Ant
- Automated deploy

The quickest and easiest way to deploy (from a practical point of view) is definitely the Admin Console or Enterprise Manager console. To do a quick deployment without having too much knowledge about the deployment process is the best way to make use of these tools. When your company has lots of applications to be deployed, or when applications change frequently, such as during integration tests, it's better to use a more advanced tool to set up automated or scripted deployments.

The WebLogic Admin Console

The WebLogic Admin Console is by far the easiest way to do a quick deployment.

First of all, you should have a packaged `ear` or `war` file ready somewhere on your own computer, or you can upload it to the WebLogic Server environment (on `*NIX`, you could use an SCP or FTP client). With this client, you login in as the WebLogic Server software owner (usually named Oracle) and transfer the file into a directory from which you deploy the application into Oracle WebLogic.

1. Prepare your WebLogic Server.

    Navigate to the **Domain Structure** panel, and click on **Deployments**. A list of installed applications and libraries appear in the right pane. Click on **Install** (in Production Mode, first lock a session).

2. Upload your packaged file or locate it on the WebLogic Server.

3. You can upload your packaged file or locate it if it's already on the WebLogic Server. Click on **Next**.

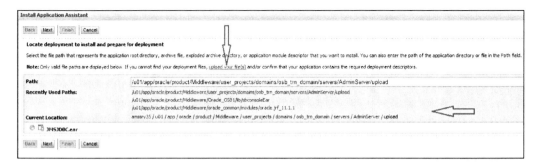

4. In the next screen, decide to install it as an application or a shared library that can act as a reference to other applications. All these applications can make use of one centralized library stored in the WebLogic Server configuration.

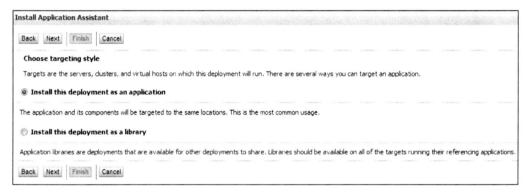

5. Choose a target for your application.

   Next, you should choose a target in which your application will run. In this case, the target is a Managed Server; your application will run inside the JVM of the Managed Server. It's better not to target the Admin Server; the Admin Server should be used for administrative tasks.

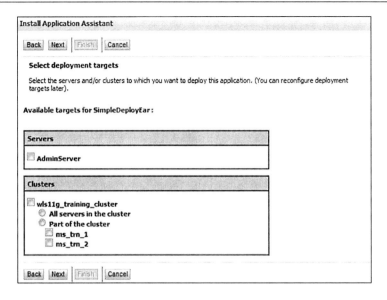

6. Review and install.

A final screen appears in which you can set the application name and special options such as security, but in this simple deployment we leave these option as the default.

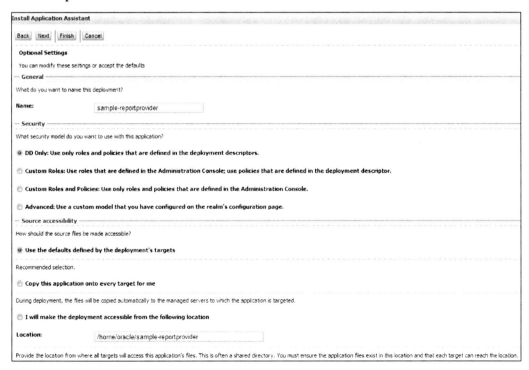

After this, you can click on **Finish**, or **Next** to review. When installation is successful, and the target Managed Server is running, your application will be started and appear in the NEW state. You can start the application from the **Deployments** screen. In Production Mode you first have to activate your configuration before starting.

An application start failure can happen and it can have many different causes, such as flaws in the code, version difference in classes or libraries between the application and WebLogic, or configuration issues that the application depends on. For instance, if the application relies on a resource of the WebLogic server, such as a JDBC connection or connection-factory, it might fail to start, when the JDBC (or other resource needed) has not been created. In more advanced deployments, these resources can be created along with the deployment of the application, but if not, you should be aware of it, and ask your developer if there are additional resources needed, so that you can create them and configure them with the proper specifications.

You can test a deployed application using the Administration Console, by selecting and expanding the contents of the application.

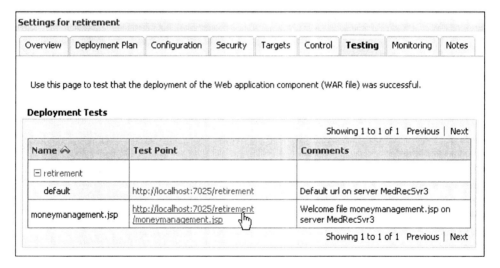

This deployment can also be done through Enterprise Manager Console. The process is quite the same as in the Admin Console.

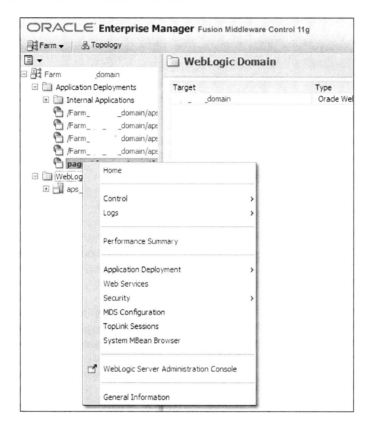

The Fusion Middleware Enterprise Manager Console is an extension on the Admin Console, but is not installed by default with a standard WebLogic domain configuration. However, if you use it, it has a very sophisticated tool to use for your deployment.

Weblogic.Deployer tool

A command-line tool used within WebLogic Server is the Weblogic.Deployer command-line interface. It's a JAVA class that can be used by administrators or developers. With this tool you can create or configure your own deployment interface (by scripts, or by a tool such as Hudson or Maven).

Some examples of how to use this tool are as follows:

- Deploy application on admin server:

```
java weblogic.Deployer -adminurl url -username username -password
password -name myapp -deploy app.ear
```

- Deploy individual modules in application to different targets:

```
java weblogic.Deployer -adminurl url -username username -password
password -name myapp -targets server1 –deploy app.ear
```

- Undeploy application from specified targets:

```
java weblogic.Deployer -adminurl url -username username -password
password -name myapp -undeploy -targets server1,server2..
```

- Redeploy application on current targets:

```
java weblogic.Deployer -adminurl url -username username -password
password  -name myapp -redeploy
```

- Redeploy individual module in an application:

```
java weblogic.Deployer -adminurl url -username username -password
password -name myapp -redeploy -targets moduleA@serverA,moduleA@
serverB
```

To use Java, you should set the `JAVA_HOME` and include the Java executable in your `PATH` variable. You can do this by running the `setDomainEnv` script. The `setDomainEnv` script is located in the `<DOMAIN_HOME>/bin` directory.

WLST (WebLogic Scripting Tool)

Doing a deployment with WLST can be useful if you like to script and automate your deployment.

WLST uses two objects for the deployment process, which are:

WLSTPlan: This enables changes to be made to an application deployment plan after loading an application.

WLSTProgress: This is used to check the progress of a deployment. Commands within this object are:

- deploy
- distributeApplication
- redeploy
- startApplication
- stopApplication
- updateApplication

A sample of a simple WLST script for deployment is as follows:

```
# Connect to the server
print 'Connecting to server  .... '
connect('weblogic','welcome1','t3://localhost:7001')
appname = "mbeanlister"
applocation = "<filelocation of app>"
# Start deploy
print 'Deploying application ' + appname
deploy(appname, applocation, targets='myserver',
        planPath=<filelocation of plan>)
print 'Done Deploying the application '+ appname
exit()
```

Autodeploy

By default, the autodeployment feature is enabled only if the domain is not running in production mode. When enabled, the Admin Server monitors its `autodeploy` folder for new, updated, or removed applications.

Auto-deployment can be useful when performing continuous integration tests. Applications get tested, changed in the code, transferred to the `autodeploy` directory, and the new version is already available again with the new or enhanced functionalities.

The directory `<WL_HOME>/user_projects/domains/domain/autodeploy` is the directory where packaged applications can be placed.

The deployment plan

Deployment plans are part of the JSR-88 deployment standard, although not explicitly stated in this standard.

A *deployment plan* is an XML document that defines an application's WebLogic Server deployment configuration for a specific WebLogic environment. This was introduced since WebLogic 9. A deployment plan is not a part of an application package, but can apply changes to deployment properties stored in the application's existing WebLogic Server deployment descriptors (such as `weblogic.xml`). As an administrator, you can use deployment plans to change an application's configuration for a specific environment, without modifying existing J2EE or WebLogic-specific deployment descriptors. Multiple deployment plans can be used to reconfigure a single application for deployment to multiple, differing WebLogic server environments.

The deployment plan contains a set of search and replace rules that are applied to override the deployment descriptors in the archive, after unpacking and before actually deploying (or as an update to an existing application deployment).

```
<deployment-plan xmlns="http://www.bea.com/ns/weblogic/deployment-
plan" xmlns:xsi="http://www.w3.org/2001/XMLSchema-instance"
xsi:schemaLocation="http://www.bea.com/ns/weblogic/deployment-plan
http://www.bea.com/ns/weblogic/deployment-plan/1.0/deployment-plan.
xsd" global-variables="false">
  <application-name>helloworld.ear</application-name>
  <variable-definition>
<!--  add the wsdl var    -->
    <variable>
      <name>wsdlUrl</name>
      <value>http://localhost:7001/ws_helloworld/
HelloWorldServicePort?WSDL</value>
    </variable>
<module-descriptor external      <root-element>web-app</root-element>
      <uri>WEB-INF/web.xml</uri>

<!-- replace the wsdl url with the deployment url -->
      <variable-assignment>
        <name>wsdlUrl</name>
        <xpath>/web-app/context-param/[param-name="wsdlUrl"]/param-
value</xpath>
        <operation>replace</operation>
      </variable-assignment>
    </module-descriptor>
  </module-override>
  <config-root>app.ear\plan</config-root>
</deployment-plan>
```

In the WebLogic Console, you can specify the deployment plan when you update your application. You also could update your plan, by updating the application in the WebLogic Admin Console.

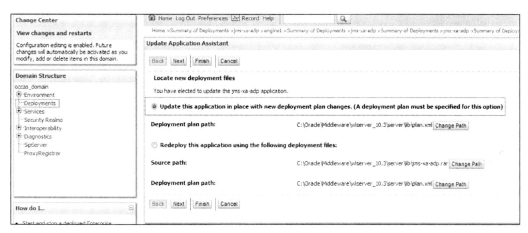

If you yet don't have a plan for your application, library, or any other module, you can generate a plan using the `weblogic.PlanGenerator` command. The following are the available options:

- `-plan`: Name of the plan

- `-dependencies`: Export all dependency properties that resolve external resource references (default)

- `-declarations`: Export all properties that declare a resource to other applications and modules

- `-configurables`: Export all editable configurables except dependencies and declarations

- `-dynamics`: Export all configurables that be changed on the fly, without needing to redeploy the application

- `-all`: Export all parameters

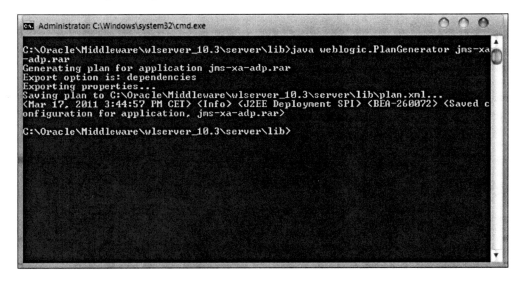

The generated plan looks similar to the following block of code:

```
?xml version='1.0' encoding='UTF-8'?>
<deployment-plan xmlns="http://xmlns.oracle.com/WebLogic/deployment-
plan" xmlns:xsi="http://www.w3.org/2001/XMLSchema-instance"
xsi:schemaLocation="http://xmlns.oracle.com/weblogic/deployment-plan
http://xmlns.oracle.com/weblogic/deployment-plan/1.0/deployment-plan.
xsd" global-variables="false">
  <application-name>jms-xa-adp.rar</application-name>
  <module-override>
    <module-name>jms-xa-adp.rar</module-name>
```

```
    <module-type>rar</module-type>
    <module-descriptor external="false">
      <root-element>weblogic-connector</root-element>
      <uri>META-INF/weblogic-ra.xml</uri>
    </module-descriptor>
    <module-descriptor external="false">
      <root-element>connector</root-element>
      <uri>META-INF/ra.xml</uri>
    </module-descriptor>
    <module-descriptor external="true">
      <root-element>wldf-resource</root-element>
      <uri>META-INF/weblogic-diagnostics.xml</uri>
    </module-descriptor>
  </module-override>
  <config-root>C:\Users\michel_s\AppData\Local\Temp\Michel_s\.\config\
deployments\jms-xa-adp.rar\plan</config-root>
</deployment-plan>
```

In this case, we only exported the main descriptors, but with the -all option, you will export all configurable items; now you can change specific properties that need to be changed. In that case an update with the new deployment plan is enough; you don't have to fully undeploy your application to make adjustments, and then do a full new deployment.

Of course, there are a whole lot more features and knowledge about deployment strategies and tools. There is unfortunately no room to handle them all, but I'd like to discuss one nice feature: parallel application versions.

Handling parallel application versions and retirement

If you would like to deploy a new version of your application, but don't want to disturb the user working, you could choose to use parallel application versions.

The current version can continue to run to ensure uninterrupted application availability, either for a specified period of time, or until all existing sessions have completed. As soon as the new version is available, new sessions will be directed to this new version. At that point, different users can see different versions of the application at the same time!

The application version is defined through a property in the application's `manifest.mf` file. Unversioned applications cannot run in parallel.

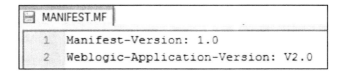

In the WebLogic Admin, you can specify a retirement period for the old version, based on finishing current sessions or setting a time period; the default is immediate.

In this case, no user will notice any outage of the application, no work will be lost, and no connections will be broken. This strategy can be useful only for any application code changes. If there are changes outside the application, this method is not enough to avoid outage.

Summary

In this chapter, you have learned the basics of deployment, how WebLogic handles deployments, which tools an administrator can use for deployment, and some strategies about how to approach the deployment process.

This is definitely not all, but it gives you a start point to think about how to handle these techniques in your own company. It doesn't matter which tool, method, or system your company uses, WebLogic can handle them all.

Now, what's an application if it can't interface with the outside world?

In *Chapter 1, Oracle WebLogic: Your First Step into a Middleware World!*, we saw a brief overview about the many available JEE resources; let's discuss some of them in the next chapter.

7
Connecting to the Outside World: JDBC and JMS

The key project of FinanceFiction is going very well!! Your manager seems very happy for the past few weeks. He received many positive responses from his superiors and the board. So your manager has invited the CEO and CTO to come and look at some live testing in the next test phase.

There is still a lot of work to do. The testing environment must be created. Up till now, the developers have used their own test data. But now it is time to load real production data into the backend test systems and databases.

It is your task to configure the WebLogic middleware environment, so it can smoothly handle all data traffic between the newly created and deployed applications and the backend systems without any data loss.

No big deal, huh?

WebLogic resources

The two important resources WebLogic provides are the **Java Database Connectivity (JDBC)** interface and the **JAVA Messaging Service (JMS)**.

Databases are very important to store loads of data that have to be available at any time and as fast as it can be delivered, so your JDBC setup in WebLogic plays an important role in this part.

About JMS, messaging is also very important when you want to have guaranteed delivery of messages between systems.

Both the subjects will be discussed in the coming pages.

JDBC

JDBC stands for **Java Database Connectivity**. JDBC is a Java interface for Java applications running SQL code against any database. It provides methods for querying and updating data in a database.

The Java Database Connectivity (JDBC) specifications:

- A mechanism for accessing and updating a database.
- Provides transparency to any kind of database vendor. Many vendors are supported (IBM DB2, Oracle, and Informix).
- Requires the use of a *driver*.

JDBC drivers are supplied by WebLogic Server or by your database vendor.

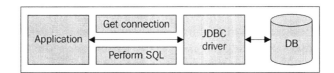

A simple connection-schematic overview:

In 1997, SUN Microsystems provided this interface with the release of their Java Development Kit (JDK 1.1).

With JDBC, an application can access virtually any database and run on any platform with a Java Virtual Machine (JVM). That is, with JDBC, it is not necessary to write one program to access a Sybase database, another to access an Oracle database, another to access an IBM DB2 database, and so on. You can write a single program using the JDBC API.

JDBC database connections use a driver mechanism that translates the JDBC calls to native database calls. Although most available drivers are fully written in Java (Type 4) and are thus platform-independent, some drivers (Type 2) use native libraries and are targeted to specific platforms. Native libraries are OS specific.

How does JDBC work

A **Datasource object** is used to establish connections. Although the Driver Manager can also be used to establish a connection, connecting through a Datasource object is the preferred method.

A **Connection object** controls the connection to the database. An application can alter the behavior of a connection by invoking the methods associated with this object. An application uses the connection object to create statements.

Statement, **PreparedStatement**, and **CallableStatement** objects are used for executing SQL statements. A PreparedStatement object is used when an application plans to reuse a statement multiple times. The application prepares the SQL it plans to use. Once prepared, the application can specify values for parameters in the prepared SQL statement. The statement can be executed multiple times with different parameter values specified for each execution. A CallableStatement is used to call stored procedures that return values. The CallableStatement has methods for retrieving the return values of the stored procedure.

A **ResultSet** object contains the results of a query. A ResultSet is returned to an application when a SQL query is executed by a statement object. The ResultSet object provides methods for iterating through the results of the query.

WebLogic JDBC

The WebLogic implementation of JDBC consists of the following component:

- Data sources:
  - ° Enable database connectivity using a dynamic pool of reusable connections
  - ° Are to be managed by the application server
  - ° Can be obtained by applications from the WebLogic Server's JNDI tree
  - ° Use a dynamic pool of reusable database connections

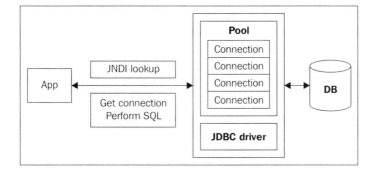

WebLogic Server can manage your database connectivity through JDBC data sources. Each data source that you configure contains a pool of database connections that are created when the data source instance is created—when it is deployed or targeted, or at server startup. The connection pool can grow or shrink dynamically to accommodate the demand.

Applications look up a data source on the Java Naming and Directory Interface (JNDI) tree or in the local application context (`java:comp/env`), depending on how you configure and deploy the object, and then request a database connection. When finished with the connection, the application uses the close operation on the connection, which simply returns the connection to the connection pool in the data source.

WebLogic Server data sources allow connection information, such as the JDBC driver, the database location (URL), and the username and password to be managed and maintained in a single location, without requiring the application to worry about these details.

Datasource configuration is stored in a XML file at `<DOMAIN_HOME>/config/jdbc`.

All WebLogic JDBC module files must end with the `-jdbc.xml` suffix, such as `examples-demo-jdbc.xml`. They have a reference tag in the `config.xml`.

WebLogic JDBC drivers

The WebLogic Type 4 JDBC drivers are installed with Oracle WebLogic Server in the `<WL_HOME>/server/lib` folder. Driver class files are included in the manifest classpath in `weblogic.jar`, so the drivers are automatically added to your classpath on the server.

The WebLogic Type 4 JDBC drivers are installed by default when you perform a complete installation of Oracle WebLogic Server. If you choose a custom installation, ensure that the WebLogic JDBC Drivers checkbox is selected. If this option is deselected, the drivers are not installed.

Connection pool

Oracle WebLogic Server opens JDBC connections to the database during the WebLogic startup process and adds the connections to the pool. This is faster than creating a new connection on demand. The size of the pool is dynamic and can be fine-tuned.

Usually, making a DBMS connection is a very slow process. When Oracle WebLogic Server starts, connections from the connection pools are opened and are available to all clients. When a client closes a connection from a connection pool, the connection is returned to the pool and is available for other clients; the connection itself is not closed. There is little cost in opening and closing pool connections. The alternative is for application code to create its own JDBC connections as needed. A DBMS runs faster when it can use dedicated connections than when it has to handle every individual connection attempt at runtime.

Connection information, such as the JDBC driver class name, the database location (URL), and the username and password can be managed in one location using the Administration Console. Application developers can obtain a connection without having to worry about these details.

Limiting the number of DBMS connections is also important if you have a licensing limitation for DBMS connections or a resource concern.

Creating a Data Source with the Administration Console

The first thing an administrator will encounter is the creation of a Data Source. This could be done in the Administration Console.

1. Select **Data Sources** in the **Domain Structure**:

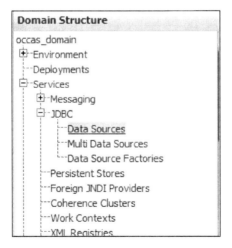

2. Click on **New**.

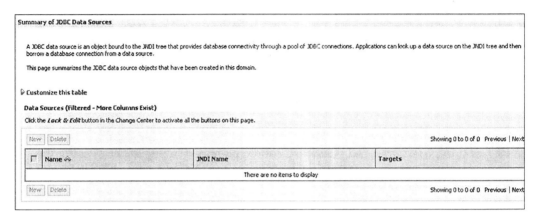

3. Fill in the details like **Name** and **JNDI Name**. JNDI name should be something similar to `jdbc/<datasourcename>`.

4. Select which driver is needed. For products like the Oracle SOA Suite, you often need an XA driver.

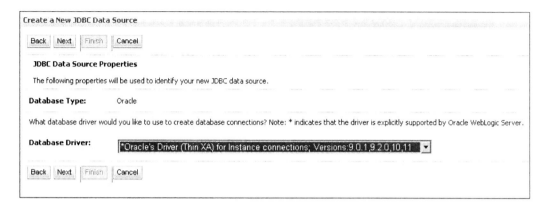

5. Provide the name and the TCP port of the database, and the database server name. It will ask your DBA whether it requires an Instance or Service connection.

In more complicated architectures, databases are located in another tier (usually called a Data Tier) than your WebLogic Server (usually the Application Tier). Contact your network administrator if the firewall route and port are set from WebLogic to the database. The user schema which you specify in your JDBC should be created in the database. If username or password is incorrect, or it's not there, you will probably get an ORA-01017 error.

Provide database account username and password.

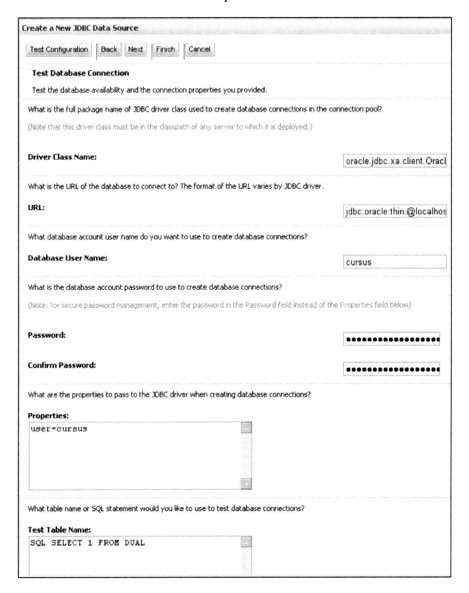

Now, you can test the configuration. When you're done, complete the configuration by pressing the **Finish** button.

Some advanced settings

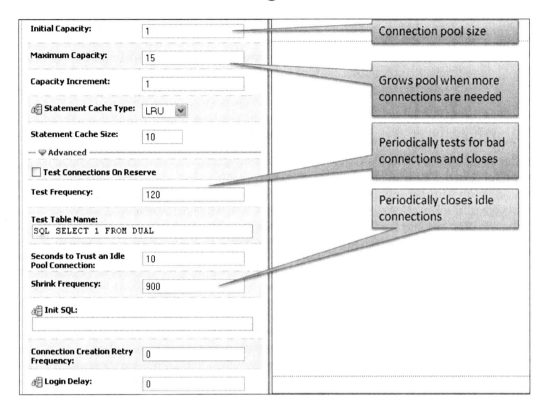

These settings could be important to set, but always monitor your JDBC first before you make any changes, and look at their behavior. All these settings can have a huge impact, so always be careful.

Here are some of these settings explained:

- **Initial Capacity**: This is the number of physical connections to create when deploying the connection pool.

- **Maximum Capacity**: This is the maximum number of physical connections that this connection pool can contain. For optimal performance, set the value of Initial Capacity equal to the value for Maximum Capacity. Be aware that this disables the dynamic resizing.

- **Capacity Increment**: When there are no more available physical connections to satisfy connection requests, Oracle WebLogic Server creates this number of additional physical connections and adds them to the connection pool up to the maximum capacity.

- **Test Frequency**: This is the time in seconds that Oracle WebLogic Server tests the unused connections. This requires that you specify a Test Table Name. In an Oracle database, you could use DUAL for this purpose.

Monitoring and testing a Data Source

After you create a JDBC Data Source and target it to one or more servers, you can monitor it in the Administration Console. Locate and select your new Data Source and click on **Monitoring | Statistics** tab. Statistics are displayed for each deployed instance of the Data Source. Optionally, click **Customize this table** to change the columns displayed in the Statistics table. For example, some of the available columns (not displayed by default) include:

- **Active Connections Current Count**: The number of connections currently in use by applications

- **Active Connections Average Count**: The average number of active connections from the time that the data source was deployed

- **Connections Total Count**: The cumulative total number of database connections created in this Data Source from the time the Data Source was deployed

- **Current Capacity**: The current count of JDBC connections in the connection pool in the Data Source

- **Highest Num Available**: The highest number of database connections that were available at any time in this instance of the Data Source from the time the Data Source was deployed

- **Waiting for Connection High Count**: The highest number of application requests concurrently waiting for a connection from this instance of the Data Source

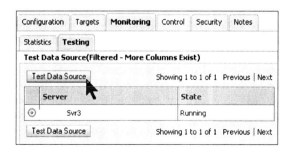

JMS

JMS stands for Java Message Service and can be categorized under
Message-Oriented Middleware (MOM).

The message-oriented middleware became widely used when providers created
architectures that could operate in a standard way on a variety of platforms and
enable asynchronous communication between applications. These providers
gained popularity in enabling integration of mainframes and personal computers.

Even though there is much variety in MOM products, they fall into one of the
following categories:

- Point-to-point
- Publish/Subscribe
- Request-reply

An enterprise messaging system enables applications to asynchronously
communicate with one another through messages. A message is a request, report,
or event that contains information needed to coordinate communication between
different applications.

JMS messaging models

JMS supports the point-to-point (PTP) and publish/subscribe messaging models.
The models are very similar, except the following:

- The PTP messaging model enables delivery of a message to exactly
  one recipient.

  When using a PTP queue, multiple message producers can put messages
  onto a single queue. The queue serializes the messages in a linear order. Multiple receivers can pull messages off the queue—in FIFO order. The oldest
  message on the queue is the first one to be taken off.

  A message can be delivered only to one receiver. Receivers are also referred
  to as consumers.

  A request-reply messaging model is more suited to a synchronous messaging
  environment where the requester and replier are in conversational mode—
  the requester waits for a response from the replier before continuing work.

- In publish/subscribe, you have multiple consumers that subscribe to certain messages (named topics). When the producer publishes its message to the topic, all consumers/subscribers receive the message.

  By decoupling a subscriber from the publisher, the subscriber does not have to determine whether its publisher is active. If the message-oriented middleware server is executing, the needs of both the publishers and the subscribers are met.

Oracle WebLogic JMS features

Oracle WebLogic Server JMS uses its built-in support for JDBC and JDBC connection pools to persist JMS messages in a database, but the default is file-based persistency.

Oracle WebLogic supports transactional message delivery. Transactional message delivery gives the developer the ability to put a JMS session into a transaction context. In Oracle WebLogic JMS, the message is not visible or available for consumption until the transaction is committed. A session can optionally roll back the transaction, which has the transaction "drop" the messages it had previously buffered.

The following diagram shows a typical WebLogic JMS architecture:

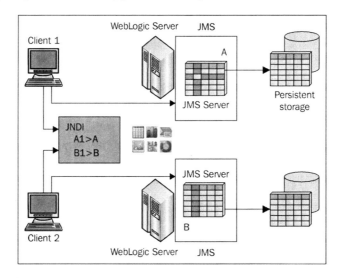

The main components of the WebLogic JMS Server architecture include:

- JMS servers that can host a defined set of modules and any associated persistent storage that resides on a WebLogic Server instance. JMS server configuration is stored in the domain `config.xml` file.

- Client JMS applications that either produce messages to destinations or consume messages from destinations.

- Java Naming and Directory Interface (JNDI), which provides a resource lookup facility. JMS resources such as connection factories and destinations are configured with a JNDI name. The runtime implementations of these resources are then bound to JNDI using the given names.

- WebLogic persistent storage (file store or JDBC-accessible) for storing persistent message data.

WebLogic JMS tasks

You, as an administrator, would be asked to do the following tasks:

- Creating and monitoring JMS servers and JMS stores
- Create JMS modules
- Creating connection factories
- Creating and monitoring destinations

Creating and monitoring JMS servers

You can create and configure a JMS server by using the Administration Console. To create a JMS server, perform the following steps:

1. In the Services node in Domain Structure in the left panel, click **JMS Servers**.

2. Click **New** at the JMS Servers table.

3. Enter values for the following configuration parameters:

    ° **Name:** The name of the JMS server.

    ° **Persistent Store**: The backing store used by destinations. A value of none means that the JMS server will use the default persistent store that is configured on each targeted WLS instance. It can be file-based or database. Database is usually a bit slower, but has some other advantages. There is less message loss on server outs. Applications can take advantage of any high-availability or failover solutions offered by the database. On file-based, this could be more difficult to guarantee as you are using shared disks only.

4. Then target a JMS server.

5. When you specify that you want to create a new store in step 3, the **Select store type** page appears. You can select **File Store** or **JDBC Store**.

6. If you specify File Store, the **File Store Properties** page appears. When creating a File Store for the JMS Persistent store, the path name to the directory must exist on your system, so be sure to create it before completing this page.

7. If you selected JDBC Store, in the **Create New JDBC Store** page, select a configured JDBC data source or configure a new JDBC data source for the store. You cannot configure a JDBC data source that is configured to support global transactions, because WebLogic JMS supports global transactions for both file and JDBC store.

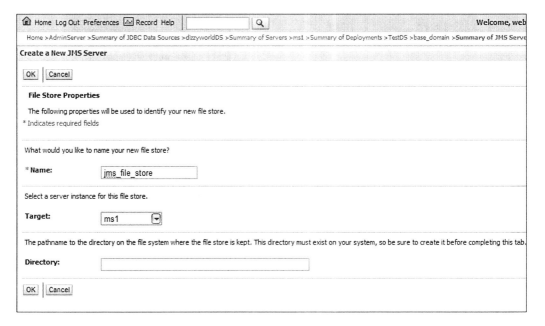

8. You can monitor the runtime statistics for an active JMS server. From the **Monitoring** tab, you can also access runtime information for a JMS server's destinations, transactions, connections, and server session pools.

9. Go to **Expand Services | Messaging** and click **JMS Servers**. Select a JMS server.

10. Click the **Monitoring** tab. By default, a Monitoring subtab is displayed, which provides general statistics for all destinations on every JMS server in the domain. These statistics include the number and size of messages processed by the JMS server.

11. The **Active Destinations** tab displays the statistics for each active JMS destination for the domain.

12. The **Active Transactions** tab displays all active JMS transactions for the domain. For troubleshooting, you can force commits or rollbacks on selected transactions. Simply select a transaction, and then click either the **Force Commit** or **Force Rollback** button.

13. The **Active Connections** tab displays all active client JMS connections for the domain. For troubleshooting, you can destroy the selected connections. Simply select a connection, and then click the **Destroy** button above the table.

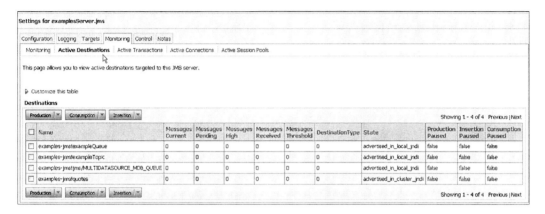

The available columns include:

- **Messages Current**: The current number of messages in the destination. This does not include the pending messages
- **Messages Pending**: The number of pending messages in the destination
- **Messages High**: The peak number in the destination since the last reset
- **Messages Received**: Number of messages received in this destination since the last reset
- **Messages Threshold**: Amount of time in the threshold condition since the last reset
- **Consumers Current**: The current number of consumers accessing this destination

Create JMS modules

Configuration of JMS resources such as queues, topics, and connection factories are within JMS modules. An administrator can create and manage JMS modules as:

- Global system resources
- Global standalone modules
- Modules packaged with an enterprise application

JMS configuration resources, such as destinations and connection factories, are stored outside of the WebLogic domain configuration file as module descriptor files of an application. JMS modules do not include the JMS server definitions.

The JMS system modules must be targeted to one or more Oracle WebLogic Server instances. The targetable resources that are defined in a system module must also be targeted to a JMS server or the Oracle WebLogic Server instances within the scope of a parent module's targets.

Creating a JMS System Module

In the following screenshot you can see how to specifiy a new JMS Module:

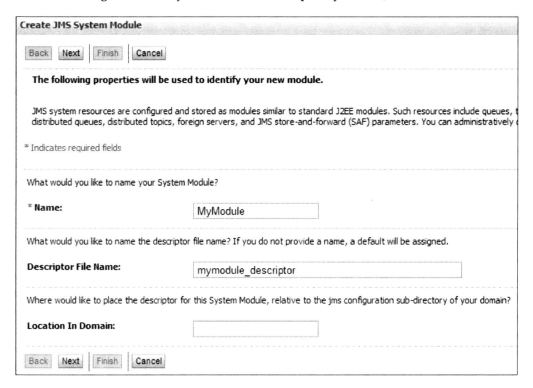

The configuration of JMS resources, such as destinations and connection factories, are stored outside of the WebLogic domain configuration file as module descriptor files, such as the `weblogic-jms.xsd` schema.

The JMS system modules must be targeted to one or more Oracle WebLogic Server instances or to a cluster. The resources that are defined in a system module must also be targeted to a JMS server or WebLogic Server instances.

You can package JMS modules using integrated development environment (IDE) or a development tool that supports the editing of an XML descriptor file. You then deploy and manage modules using the JSR 88-based tools, such as the `weblogic.Deployer` utility or the WebLogic Administration Console.

The deployment of packaged JMS modules follows the same model as all the other components of an application: individual modules can be deployed to a single server, a cluster, or individual members of a cluster.

Besides the modules, there is also a component called **Subdeployment**. A subdeployment for JMS destinations is a mechanism by which queues and topics, and connection factories are grouped and targeted to a single JMS server. Queues and topics depend on the JMS servers they are targeted to the management of persistent messages, durable subscribers, and message paging.

For example, if you want to re-locate a group of queues with a connection factory that is targeted to a specific JMS server, you can associate the queues with the subdeployment the connection factory belongs to, provided that the connection factory is not already targeted to multiple JMS servers.

JMS modules are application-related definitions that are independent of the domain environment. You create and manage JMS resources either as system modules or application modules.

JMS application modules are a WebLogic-specific extension of Java EE modules and can be deployed either with a Java EE application (as a packaged resource) or as standalone modules that can be made globally available. Application modules are owned and modified by WebLogic developers, who package JMS resource modules with the application's EAR file.

During the process of deploying a JMS application, you link the application components to the environment-specific JMS resource definitions, such as the Managed Server instances, and the location to use for persisting JMS messages.

With modular deployment of JMS resources, you can promote your application and the required JMS configuration from environment to environment, such as from a testing environment to a production environment, without opening an enterprise application file (such as an EAR file) or a standalone JMS module, and without extensive manual JMS reconfiguration.

Creating connection factories, queues, and topics

Within each JMS module, the connection factory resource names must be unique. All the connection factory JNDI names in any JMS module must be unique across an entire WebLogic domain.

When you create a JMS Module, you can go on and create additional destinations.

A JMS destination identifies a queue (point-to-point) or topic (publish/subscribe) resource within a JMS module. Each queue and topic resource is targeted to a specific JMS server. A JMS server's primary responsibility for its targeted destinations is to maintain information about the persistent store that is used for any persistent messages that arrive on the destinations and to maintain the states of the durable subscribers created on the destinations.

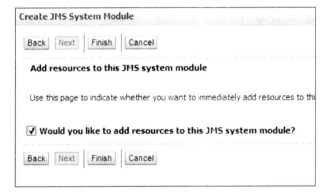

Connection factories

Connection factories are resources that enable JMS clients to create JMS connections. WebLogic JMS provides preconfigured default connections. You can also configure one or more connection factories to create connections with predefined options that better suit your application.

When connection factory options are modified at runtime, only the incoming messages are affected; stored messages are not affected.

To create a new Connection Factory, click on the **JMS Module**, and then add a JMS Destination. The **Connection Factory** will be the first one in the list

You can give it the name and JNDI:

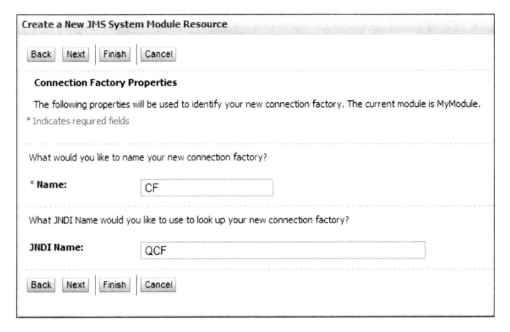

After this, you can target it to a Managed Server instance or Subdeployment.

Topics and Queues

The queues (point-to-point) or topics (publish/subscribe) are also grouped as JMS destinations. After configuring a JMS server, configure one or more queue or topic destinations for each JMS server. You configure destinations explicitly or by configuring a destination template that can be used to define multiple destinations with similar attribute settings.

A JMS destination identifies a queue (point-to-point) or topic (publish/subscribe) resource within a JMS module.

The main difference between a Topic and a Queue is that a Topic is synchronous and a Queue asynchronous.

In the same screen to create a new Connection Factory, you also can create these resources.

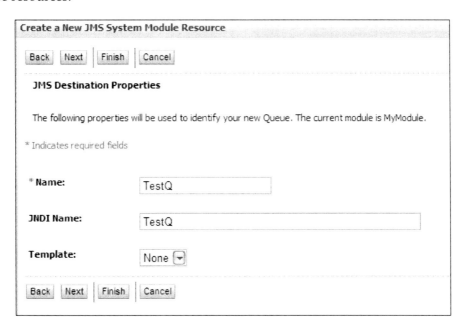

Summary

Wow! Testdata is flowing through your systems right now. You've set up all the needed resources.

At one time you received a worrying call from the datacentre OPS that a power failure took place.

Your boss posed as the usual stressful manager he should be, ready to escalate to the highest level, because he thought we lost all the entire data.

But you knew better of course and because you've configured your JEE resources in a proper way, no data at all was lost and you showed your boss that there was nothing to worry about.

But after this power failure, you would have to lift your WebLogic Server to a higher level, so let's Cluster them!!!!

8

Making your WebLogic Mission-Critical: Clustering

Nowadays, computers can't be left out of our society. Almost everyone in our modern society has some link with a computer or computer network. All our personal, financial, and government-related data, or perhaps even an account at an Internet shop, is stored in highly advanced computers. These systems should serve millions of people, without running out of resources and becoming a bad performing system. Also a lot of data needs to be available at any time and at any place. Downtime and bad performing systems are not an option in our 24-hour economy.

So, what could be a solution to fulfill all the above needs? I guess you already have the answer: Clustering.

Also your company, FinanceFiction, has to meet the satisfaction of all its customers. In this case, you've introduced Oracle WebLogic Server's solution.

Definition of a cluster

An Oracle WebLogic server cluster consists of one or more Oracle WebLogic Managed Server instances running simultaneously and working together to provide increased scalability and reliability. A cluster appears to clients as one Oracle WebLogic Server instance. The server instances that constitute a cluster can run on one machine or on different machines.

By replicating the services provided by one instance, an enterprise system achieves a fail-safe and scalable environment. It is good practice to set all the servers in a cluster to provide the same services.

You can increase a cluster's capacity by adding server instances to the cluster on an existing machine, or by adding machines to the cluster to host the incremental server instances.

The clustering support for different types of applications is as follows:

- For Web applications, the cluster architecture enables replicating the HTTP session state of clients. You can balance the Web application load across a cluster by using an Oracle WebLogic server proxy plug-in or an external load-balancer.

- For Enterprise JavaBeans (EJBs) and Remote Method Invocation (RMI) objects, clustering uses the object's replica-aware stub. When a client makes a call through a replica-aware stub to a service that has failed, the stub detects the failure and retries the call on another replica.

- For JMS applications, clustering supports cluster-wide transparent access to destinations from any member of the cluster.

Benefits of clustering

A WebLogic Server cluster provides the following benefits:

- **Scalability**: The capacity of a cluster is not limited to one server or one machine. Servers can be added to the cluster dynamically to increase capacity. If more hardware is needed, a new server instance can be added on a new host.

- **Load balancing**: The distribution of jobs and associated communications across the computing and networking resources in your environment can be evenly distributed, depending on your environment. Even Distributions include round-robin and random algorithms.

- **Failover ability of applications**: Distribution of applications and their objects on multiple servers enables easier failover of the applications.

- **Availability**: A cluster uses the redundancy of multiple servers for clients that fail. The same service can be provided on multiple servers in a cluster. If one server fails, another can take over. The capability to execute failover from a failed server to a functioning server increases the availability of the application to clients.

In this case, it makes Oracle WebLogic a redundant, scalable, and reliable system to host applications and their resources.

Components that can be clustered

Clustering serves all the earlier mentioned capabilities for the following components that run in a WebLogic server environment:

- Servlets
- JSP
- EJB
- Remote Method Invocation (RMI) objects
- Java Messaging Service (JMS) destinations
- Java Database Connectivity (JDBC) connections

Basic recommended architecture

The basic cluster architecture combines all Web application tiers and puts the related services (static HTTP, presentation logic, and objects) into one cluster.

This architecture has the following advantages:

- **Single point of administration**: Because one cluster hosts static HTTP pages, servlets, and EJBs, you can configure the entire Web application and deploy or undeploy objects using one administration console. You need not maintain a separate layer of Web servers (and configure Oracle WebLogic proxy plug-ins) to benefit from clustered servlets.

- **Load balancing**: Using load-balancing hardware directly in front of the Oracle WebLogic cluster enables you to use advanced load-balancing policies for access to both HTML and servlet content.

- **Better security**: Putting a firewall in front of your load-balancing hardware enables you to set up a demilitarized zone (DMZ) for your web application using minimal firewall policies.

- **Better performance**: The combined-tier architecture gives the best performance for applications in which most or all the servlets or JSPs in the presentation layer typically access objects in the object layer, such as EJBs or JDBC objects.

Look at the following diagram to see this type of architecture:

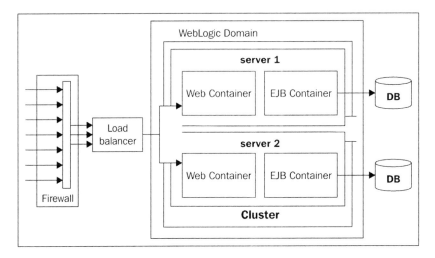

Other WebLogic clustering architecture models

- **Multi-Tier Architecture**: Application layer is deployed on two clusters: a WebLogic server cluster for the Web Layer and Presentation tier and another WebLogic server cluster for the Object Layer (EJB, RMI).

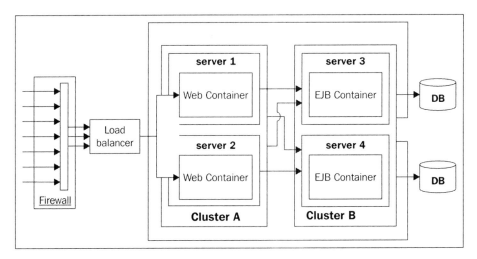

- **Basic Cluster Proxy Architecture**: This is similar to the basic cluster architecture, except that static content is hosted on HTTP servers. The two-tier proxy architecture has 2 layers, that is the Web layer and Servlet/Object layer.

The proxy architecture uses a layer of hardware and software that is dedicated to the task of providing the application's Web layer.

The physical layer of the Web servers should only provide static Web pages. Dynamic content such as servlets and JSPs are proxied via the proxy plug-in or `HttpClusterServlet` to an Oracle WebLogic server cluster that hosts servlets and JSPs for the presentation tier.

The basic cluster proxy architecture hosts the presentation and object tiers on a cluster of Oracle WebLogic server instances. This cluster can be deployed either on a single machine or on multiple separate machines. The Servlet/Object layer differs from the combined-tier cluster, in that it does not provide static HTTP content to application clients.

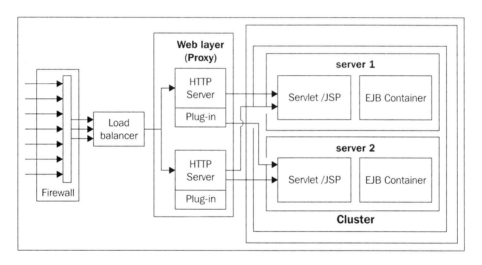

- Multi-Tier Proxy Architecture: It is like Multi-Tier Recommended Architecture, but here the Web tier is hosted on a separate Web layer with WebLogic Proxy plug-in on the WebLogic Server.

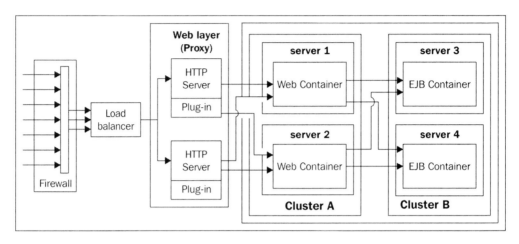

When to use Multi-Tier Recommended Architecture?

If you require more load balancing options (EJBs) or higher availability, then a Multi-Tier solution could be the best option to choose. By dividing servlets and EJBs on separate clusters, the servlet-method calls to the EJBs can be load-balanced across multiple servers.

Separating the presentation and object tiers onto separate clusters provides you with more options for distributing the load of the Web application. For example, if the application accesses HTTP and servlet content more often than EJB content, you can use a large number of Oracle WebLogic instances in the presentation tier cluster to concentrate access to a smaller number of servers that host the EJBs. Also, if your Web clients make heavy use of servlets and JSPs but access a relatively smaller set of clustered objects, then the multi-tier architecture enables you to concentrate the load of servlets and EJB objects appropriately. You may configure a servlet cluster of 10 Oracle WebLogic server instances and an object cluster of three Managed Servers, while still fully using each server's hardware resources.

WebLogic cluster communications

WebLogic server instances in a cluster communicate with one another using two basic network technologies:

- IP sockets, which are the conduits for peer-to-peer communication between clustered server instances.

- IP unicast or multicast, which is used by server instances to broadcast availability of services and heartbeats that indicate continued availability.

Unicast

When creating a new cluster, it is recommended that you use unicast for messaging within a cluster. It is much easier to configure because it does not require cross-network configuration that multicast requires. It also reduces potential network errors that can occur from multicast address conflicts.

You could consider the following if you are going to use unicast to handle cluster communications:

- All members of a cluster must use the same message type. Mixing between multicast and unicast messaging is not allowed.

- You must use multicast if you need to support a previous version of WebLogic server within your cluster.

- Individual cluster members cannot override the cluster messaging type.

- The entire cluster must be restarted to change the messaging type. Unicast uses TCP socket communication and multicast uses UDP communication. On networks where UDP is not supported, unicast must be used.

Multicast

For backwards compatibility with previous versions of Oracle WebLogic, you must use multicast for communications between clusters.

Multicast broadcasts one-to-many communications between clustered instances. WebLogic server uses IP multicast for all one-to-many communications among server instances in a cluster. Each WebLogic server instance in a cluster uses multicast to broadcast regular "heartbeat" messages. By monitoring heartbeat messages, server instances in a cluster determine when a server instance has failed (clustered server instances also monitor IP sockets as a more immediate method of determining when a server instance has failed).

IP multicast is a broadcast technology that enables multiple applications to subscribe to an IP address and port number and listen for messages. A multicast address is an IP address in the range 224.0.0.0 – 239.255.255.255.

If your cluster is divided over multiple subnets, your network must be configured to reliably transmit messages. A firewall can break IP multicast transmissions and the multicast address should not be shared with other applications. Also, multicast storms may occur, when server instances in a cluster do not process incoming messages on a timely basis, thus generating more network traffic, which causes round trips with no end.

Configuring clusters

You can use different ways to configure a cluster:

- **Administration Console**: If you have an operational domain within which you want to configure a cluster, you can use the Administration Console.
- **Configuration Wizard**: The Configuration Wizard is the recommended tool for creating a new domain with the cluster.
- **WebLogic Scripting Tool (WLST)**: You can use the WebLogic Scripting Tool in a command-line scripting interface to monitor and manage clusters.
- **Java Management Extensions (JMX)**: WebLogic server provides MBeans, that you can use to configure, monitor, and manage WebLogic server resources through JMX.
- **WebLogic Server Application Programming Interface (API)**: You can write a program to modify the configuration attributes, based on configuration application programming.

To configure a cluster with the Admin Console, perform the following steps:

1. In the Administration Console, expand **Environment** and click on **Clusters**, and then **New**.
2. Enter the name of the new cluster and select the messaging mode that you want to use for this cluster:
   - ° Unicast is the default messaging mode. Unicast requires less network configuration than multicast.
   - ° Multicast messaging mode is also available and may be appropriate in environments that use previous versions of Oracle WebLogic server. However, unicast is the preferred mode considering the simplicity of configuration and flexibility.

3. If you are using Unicast message mode, enter the Unicast broadcast channel. This channel is used to transmit messages within the cluster. If you anticipate high volume of traffic and your applications use session replication, you may prefer defining a separate channel for cluster messaging mode. If you do not specify a channel, the default channel is used.

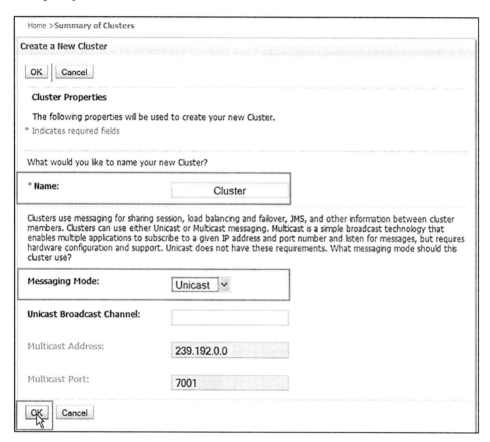

Cluster address

Each ListenAddress: ListenPort combination in the cluster address corresponds to the Managed Server and network channel that received the request. The order in which the ListenAddress: ListenPort combinations appear in the cluster address is random; the order varies from request to request.

Load balancing

The algorithm to be used for load balancing between replicated services, if none is specified for a particular service, is round-robin. The round-robin algorithm cycles in order through a list of Oracle WebLogic server instances. Weight-based load balancing improves on the round-robin algorithm by taking into account a pre-assigned weight for each server. In random load balancing, requests are routed to servers at random. This is only used for EJB clustering. These define global default and the EJB's configuration can override these.

Cluster creating with WLST

With the `cmo.createCluster` a cluster can be created within WLST. The following is a simple example of a cluster create script snippet:

```
.........

#Create and Configure a Cluster and assign the Managed Servers to that
cluster

cd('/')
create('appcluster','Cluster')
assign('Server', 'app01,app02','Cluster','appcluster')
cd('Clusters/appcluster')
set('MulticastAddress','237.0.0.101')
set('MulticastPort',7204)

#Write the domain and Close the domain template

updateDomain()
closeDomain()

exit()
```

Creating a cluster with the Configuration Wizard

When configuring a domain, you can choose to create a cluster in the domain creation process. After the domain has been created, you can use the pack and unpack command to pack the domain configuration and deploy it on all the servers where you want a Managed Server to run.

After the domain is created, you can use pack to pick-up the configuration and transfer it to a second physical host.

Syntax of the Pack command

```
pack-domain=path_of_domain-template=path_of_jar_file_to_create-
template_name="template_name" [-template_author="author"][-template_
desc="description"] [-managed=true|false][-log=log_file] [-log_
priority=log_priority]
```

```
unpack-template=path_of_jar_file-domain=path_of_domain_to_be_created
[-user_name=username] [-password=password] [-app_dir=application_
directory] [-java_home=java_home_directory] [-server_start_mode=dev|prod]
[-log=log_file] [-log_priority=log_priority]
```

Run `pack.sh` to bundle domain and templates from *Machine1* (this will create a jar file). Copy the jar file (created by using `pack.sh` command) from *Machine1* to *Machine2*. Use `unpack.sh` to create *Domain & Managed server* on *Machine2*.

Best practices in a WebLogic cluster

There are a lot of best practices about how to deal with a WebLogic cluster setup. Of course, you want to have the benefit of the cluster and not get stressed about all kinds of issues that can occur.

Hardware

You can set up a cluster on a single computer for demonstration or development, but not for production environments. Also, each physical host in a cluster should have a static IP address.

There is no built-in limit for the number of server instances in a cluster. Large multiprocessor servers can host clusters with numerous servers. The recommendation is one server instance for every two CPUs.

Administration Server

The Administration Server should join a cluster. It's dedicated to the process of administering servers. But if the Administration Server joins a cluster, there is a risk of delays in accomplishing administration tasks.

Also, do not create a separate configuration file for each server in the cluster. Keep it with the Administration Server. It will be pushed to other servers, so no need to create it separately.

IP addresses and hostnames

For a production environment, use the hostname resolved at DNS rather than IP addresses. Each server should have a unique name. The multicast address should not be used for anything other than cluster communications.

If the internal and external DNS names of a WebLogic server instance are not identical, use the `ExternalDNSName` attribute for the server instance, to define the server's external DNS name. Outside the firewall, `ExternalDNSName` should translate to the external IP address of the server.

If clients access Oracle WebLogic server over the default channel and T3, then do not set the `ExternalDNSName`, even if the internal and external DNS names of a WebLogic server instance are not identical, so as to avoid unnecessary DNS lookups.

Use the cluster address

The cluster address is used to communicate with entity and session beans by constructing the hostname portion of the request URLs. You can explicitly define the address of a cluster, or use the dynamically generated one. The cluster address should be a DNS name that maps to the IP addresses or the DNS name of each Oracle WebLogic server instance in the cluster.

You can also have Oracle WebLogic server dynamically generate an address for each new request. This gives you less configuration and ensures an accurate cluster address.

In the following screenshot, you can see where you should set the cluster address.

Firewall

While choosing the cluster architecture, be aware of the position in the network. If you choose a multi-tier architecture or even a proxy variant, firewalls should be configured for the various components in the architecture.

If you place a firewall between the Web layer and object layer in a multi-tier architecture, then it is better to use public DNS names rather than IP addresses. Binding those servers with IP addresses can cause address translation problems and prevent the servlet cluster from accessing individual server instances. For proxy architectures, you could have a single firewall between untrusted clients and the web server layer and one between the proxy layer and the cluster.

Deploying applications

When you initiate the deployment process, you specify the components to be deployed and the targets to which they will be deployed. The main difference between the way you deploy an application to a single server and a cluster lies in your choice of the target. When you intend to deploy an application to the cluster, you select the target from the list of clusters and not from the list of servers.

Ideally, all servers in a cluster should be running and available during the deployment process. Deploying applications when some members of the cluster are unavailable is not recommended.

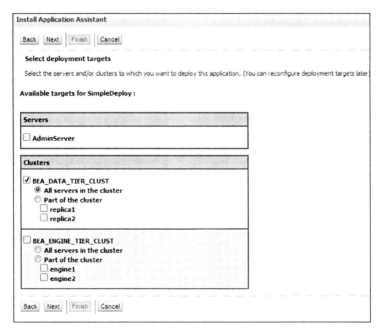

Deploying to a cluster

WebLogic clusters use the concept of two-phase deployment:

- **Phase 1**: During the first phase of deployment, components are distributed to the server instances and the deployment is validated to ensure that the application components are successfully deployed. During this phase, user requests to the application being deployed are not allowed. If failures are encountered during the distribution and validation processes, the deployment is aborted on all server instances, including those on which the validation succeeded. Files that have been staged are not removed; however, container-side changes performed during the preparation are reverted.

- **Phase 2**: After the components are distributed to targets and validated, they are fully deployed on the target server instances, and the deployed application is made available to the clients. If a failure occurs during this process, deployment to that server instance is canceled. However, a failure on one server of a cluster does not prevent successful deployment on other clustered servers.

If a cluster member fails to deploy an application, it fails at startup in order to ensure that the cluster will remain consistent, because any failure of a cluster-deployed application on a Managed Server would cause the Managed Server to abort its startup.

The two-phase commit feature enables you to avoid situations in which an application is successfully deployed on one node and not on the other. This is also referred to as **partial deployment**. One potential problem with partial deployment is that during the synchronization with other members of the cluster — when other servers in the cluster reestablish communications with the previously partitioned server instance — the user requests to the deployed applications and the attempts to create secondary sessions on that server instance may fail, causing inconsistencies in cached objects.

You can configure Oracle WebLogic server not to use relaxed or partial deployments by using the `enforceClusterConstraints` tag with `weblogic.Deployer`, WLST, or the Administration Console.

HTTP session failover in a WebLogic cluster

A technique to maintain availability can be arranged at the highest layer, the HTTP layer.

HTTP session failover

Web applications use HTTP sessions to track information in server memory for each client.

To provide high availability of Web applications, shared access to one `HttpSession` object must be provided. `HttpSession` objects can be replicated within Oracle WebLogic server by storing their data using in-memory replication, filesystem persistence, or in a database.

In a cluster, the load-balancing hardware or the proxy plug-in in Web server redirects the client requests to any available server in the WebLogic cluster. The cluster member that serves the request obtains a replica of the client's HTTP session state from the available secondary Managed Server in the cluster.

Oracle WebLogic supports several session replication strategies to recover sessions from failed servers:

- In-memory replication
- JDBC replication

Replication should be configured for each Web application within its `weblogic.xml` file.

HTTP in-memory replication

Oracle WebLogic copies a session state from one server instance to another, using in-memory replication. The primary server creates a primary session state on the server to which the client first connects and also creates a secondary replica on another Oracle WebLogic server instance in the cluster. The replica is kept up-to-date so that it can be used, if the server that hosts the Web application fails.

The WebLogic proxy plug-ins maintain a list of Oracle WebLogic server instances that host a clustered servlet or JSP and forward HTTP requests to these instances by using a simple round-robin strategy.

Oracle HTTP Server with the `mod_wl_ohs` module configured and Oracle WebLogic server with `HttpClusterServlet` are supported; Apache with the Apache Server (proxy) plug-in (`mod_weblogic`) provides an open source solution.

For in-memory replication, the application should have a descriptor in the `weblogic.xml`.

```
<session-descriptor>
   <persistent-store-type>replicated</persistent-store-type>
</session-descriptor>
```

HTTP replication can also be configured with a JDBC to store session-persistent data in a database, or by using Coherence Web replication.

Load balancer requirements

If you choose to use load-balancing hardware instead of a proxy plug-in, you must use hardware that supports SSL persistence and passive cookie persistence. Passive cookie persistence enables Oracle WebLogic to write cookies through the load balancer to the client. The load balancer, in turn, interprets an identifier in the client's cookie to maintain the relationship between the client and the primary Oracle WebLogic that hosts the HTTP session state.

Load balancing and clustering EJBs and RMIs

EJBs that are based on the 3.0 specification can be configured using annotations and deployment plans:

`weblogic-ejb-jar.xml`:

```
<stateless-clustering>
   <stateless-bean-is-clusterable>True
   </stateless-bean-is-clusterable>
   <stateless-bean-load-algorithm>random
   </stateless-bean-load-algorithm>
</stateless-clustering>
```

This is a typical example of a stateless EJB, but you can configure it for stateful EJBs. You should discuss these options with your development team.

The replication type for EJBs is In-Memory or None in the Admin Console.

Configuration

You can configure the default EJB cluster settings for your domain using the following steps:

1. Select **Environment | Clusters** within the **Domain Structure** panel of the console. Then select a specific cluster.

2. On the **General** tab, update any of the fields described as follows:

   ° *Default Load Algorithm*: The algorithm used for load balancing between replicated services, such as EJBs, if none is specified for a particular service.

   ° The round-robin algorithm cycles through a list of Oracle WebLogic server instances in order.

   ° Weight-based load balancing improves on the round-robin algorithm by taking into account a preassigned weight for each server. In random load balancing, requests are routed to servers at random.

   ° *Cluster Address*: The address used by EJB clients to connect to this cluster. This address may be either the DNS host's name that maps to multiple IP addresses or a comma-separated list of single address hostnames or IP addresses.

   ° *Number of Servers in Cluster Address*: The number of servers listed from this cluster when generating a cluster address automatically.

Migratable targets

For pinned services, services that are attached to one single Managed Server, such as JMS, you can configure migratable targets. A pinned service is available in the cluster's JNDI tree, but does not have clustering, failover, and load balancing options. So if the Managed Server instance of the service is failing, the service is lost as well. But in this case you could use migratable targets. It defines a list of server instances in the cluster that can potentially host a migratable service, such as a JMS server or the Java Transaction API (JTA) transaction recovery service. If you want to use a migratable target, configure the target server list before deploying or activating the service in the cluster. By default, WebLogic can migrate the JTA transaction recovery service or a JMS server to any other Managed Server in the cluster. You can optionally configure a list of servers in the cluster that can potentially host a pinned service. This list of servers is referred to as a migratable target, and it controls the servers to which you can migrate a service. In the case of JMS, the migratable target also defines the list of servers to which you can deploy a JMS server.

WebLogic lets you to create separate migratable targets for the JTA transaction recovery service and JMS servers. This allows you to always keep each service running on a different server in the cluster, if necessary. Also, you can configure the same selection of servers as the migratable target for both JTA and JMS, to ensure that the services remain co-located on the same server in the cluster. For each server instance, you can set up migration on the migration tab.

The following screenshot shows you the **Migration Configuration** screen:

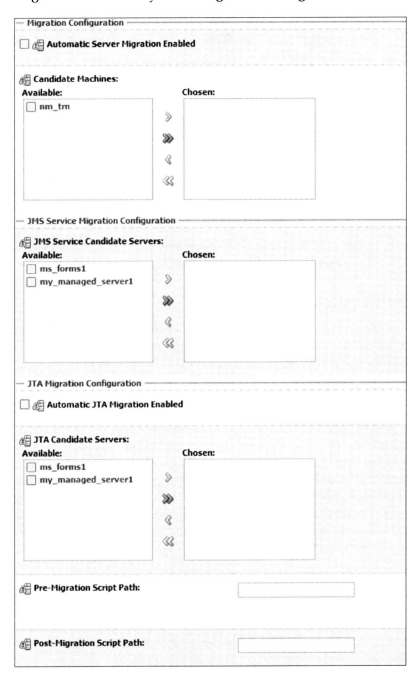

Preventing possible cluster problems

These tips could be helpful to prevent some common problems.

Check the multicast address

A problem with the multicast address is one of the most common reasons a cluster does not start or a server fails to join a cluster.

A multicast address is required for each cluster. The multicast address can be an IP number between 224.0.0.0 and 239.255.255.255, or a hostname with an IP address within that range.

You can check a cluster's multicast address and port on its **Configuration |** **Multicast** tab in the Administration Console.

For each cluster on a network, the combination of multicast address and port must be unique. If two clusters on a network use the same multicast address, they should use different ports. If the clusters use different multicast addresses, they can use the same port or accept the default port, 7001.

Before booting the cluster, make sure the cluster's multicast address and port are correct and do not conflict with the multicast address and port of any other clusters on the network.

The errors you are most likely to see if the multicast address is bad are:

- **Unable to create a multicast socket for clustering**
- **Multicast socket send error**
- **Multicast socket receive error**

You can use the multicast test tool for multicast problems when configuring a WebLogic cluster.

Syntax:

```
java utils.MulticastTest -n name -a address [-p portnumber]    [-t
timeout]   [-s send]
```

The following screenshot shows an example of a running multicast test:

```
java utils.MulticastTest -A 239.192.0.0
**** WARNING ***** WARNING ***** WARNING *****
Do NOT use the same multicast address as a running WLS cluster.


Starting test.  Hit any key to abort


Using multicast address 239.192.0.0:7001
Will send messages under the name 1311168325 every 2 seconds
Will print warning every 600 seconds if no messages are received

                I (1311168325) sent message num 1
                I (1311168325) sent message num 2
                I (1311168325) sent message num 3
                I (1311168325) sent message num 4
                I (1311168325) sent message num 5
                I (1311168325) sent message num 6
                I (1311168325) sent message num 7
```

Check the CLASSPATH value

Make sure the value of CLASSPATH is the same on all Managed Servers in the cluster. CLASSPATH is set by the setDomainEnv script. If you change the value of CLASSPATH on one Managed Server, you must change it on all Managed Servers in the cluster.

Summary

As you have seen in this chapter, clustering your WebLogic is more than an obligation to you as an administrator. But be aware, every Managed Server on a separate host needs to be charged as a full WebLogic license. So consider carefully and make good decisions when upgrading to clustering.

9

The Heart of Oracle WebLogic Server: The JVM

Oracle WebLogic Server's runtime execution environment is, as you probably know, running with Java.

Every WebLogic Server instance is running inside its own dedicated area on the physical server, getting its own allocation of processor time and memory allocation.

The area we're going to talk about in this chapter is called Java Virtual Machine (JVM).

The Java Virtual Machine (JVM)

In this chapter, there will be some secrets revealed for you! Have fun!

What is a Java Virtual Machine?

WebLogic can be used for a wide variety of applications, from small applications to very large applications. The JVM is Java's execution environment on a server or client. JVM runs on top of the machine's OS and Java programs can be executed in it.

The JVM is the environment in which Java programs execute. It is the software that is implemented on non-virtual hardware and on standard operating systems.

JVMs are available for many hardware and software platforms, also in a middleware environment such as Oracle WebLogic. The use of the same byte code for all platforms allows Java to be described as "portable". A JVM also enables features such as automated exception handling, which provides "root-cause" debugging information for every software error (exception), independent of the source code.

A JVM is distributed along with a set of standard class libraries that implement the Java Application Programming Interface (API). Appropriate APIs bundled together form the Java Runtime Environment (JRE).

Some facts about JVMs are:

- JVM was originally developed to run only Java. But as of now, it can run many languages. Languages supported by JVM are:
    ○ Ruby, with JRuby
    ○ JavaScript, with Rhino
    ○ Python, with Jython
    ○ Common Lisp, with Armed
- It makes Java code portable across operating systems
- Java Virtual Machine (JVM) runs on top of the machine's OS and Java programs can be executed in it
- JVM is a bytecode interpreter that reads and executes all Java classes
- Each OS has its own version of a virtual machine (Windows, Linux, Solaris, AIX)
- Multiple JVM providers (Sun, Bea/Oracle (JRockit), IBM)
- Runtime behavior
- Each virtual machine runs as an operating system process
- Inside JVM, work can be executed concurrently through the threading model
- Unused Java objects are automatically destroyed by the garbage collector

The Java memory model

The Java memory model is explained in the JSR 133 description. The original Java memory model, developed in 1995, was widely perceived as broken, preventing many runtime optimizations and not providing strong enough guarantees for code safety. It was updated through the Java community process, as Java Specification Request 133 (JSR-133). It tries to explain the memory model in detail and shows how the JVM deals with threads and the memory. The specification attempts to explain how incorrectly-designed applications can behave in erroneous ways because the JVM implementation might optimize the program so that it runs faster.

A memory model defines the possible scenarios and rules that govern multiple threads in a system. A memory model determines if the execution trace of a program is legally allowed by the JVM. The Java specification does not force JVM implementations to follow any particular implementation rule for program execution; this gives flexibility to the JVM implementer to provide compiler optimizations and reorganizations in the execution order. However, the memory model specifies that all implementations produce results that can be predicted by a programmer. The memory model defines the possible rules for threads and the expected behavior of multi-threaded programs so that programmers can design their programs accordingly. The responsibility of avoiding data races and deadlock conditions in threads still lies with the implementer and the programmer.

The execution environment (JRE)

Java's execution environment is also known as the Java Runtime Environment (JRE).

Programs intended to run on a JVM must be compiled into a standardized portable binary format, which typically comes in the form of `.class` files. A program may consist of many classes in different files. For easier distribution of large programs, multiple class files may be packaged together in a `.jar` file (Java archive).

The Java executable offers a standard way of executing Java code. The JVM runtime executes `.class` or `.jar` files, emulating the JVM instruction set by interpreting it, or using a just-in-time (JIT) compiler such as Oracle's Sun HotSpot. JIT compiling, not interpreting, is used in most JVMs today to get better performance. There are also ahead-of-time (AOT) compilers that enable developers to precompile class files into native code for particular platforms.

Like most virtual machines, the Java Virtual Machine has a stack-based architecture. The JVM also has low-level support for Java-like classes and methods, which amounts to a highly sophisticated memory model and capability-based architecture.

The following diagram shows *a schematic overview of a working JVM:*

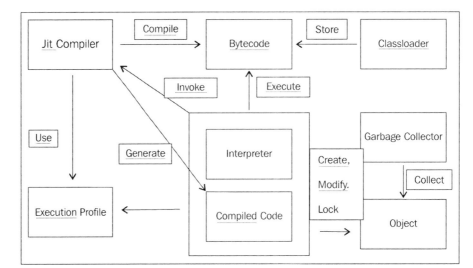

The JVM is responsible for loading and executing code. It uses a Classloader to load Java classes into the Java runtime environment. Classloaders are designed so that at start-up the JVM doesn't need to know anything about the classes that will be loaded at runtime. Almost all Java-based containers, such as EJB or servlet containers, implement custom Classloaders to support features such as hot deployment.

JVM—a bytecode interpreter

Bytecode is a step between your source code and actual machine code. The JVM is what takes the bytecode and translates it into machine code. The JVM has an instruction set, just like a real machine. The name given to this instruction set is Java bytecode. The first implementation of the Java Virtual Machine, done at Sun, emulated the Java Virtual Machine instruction set in software hosted by a handheld device. The Java Virtual Machine does not assume any particular implementation technology, hardware, or OS.

The Java Virtual Machine knows nothing of the Java programming language, but only of a particular binary format, the class file format. A class file contains Java Virtual Machine instructions (or bytecode) and a symbol table, as well as other ancillary information.

Regarding security, the Java Virtual Machine imposes strong format and structural constraints on the code in a class file. However, any language with functionality, that can be expressed in terms of a valid class file, can be hosted by the Java Virtual Machine. Attracted by a generally available, machine-independent platform, implementers of other languages are turning to the Java Virtual Machine as a delivery vehicle for their languages.

JVM threading models

Both of the JVM providers that Oracle ships with WebLogic — Sun HotSpot and BEA JRockit — use different threading models.

BEA JRockit uses both native and green (thin) threads. This is the practice where one instance of an underlying thread representation, represents several threads of a higher abstraction layer (such as `java.lang.Threads`). While this is simple and fast for uncomplicated applications, there are plenty of problems with this approach. The most serious one has to do with handling threads and the acquisition of locks. In native code, where no control can be exerted over the threads, or when threads are waiting for I/O, deadlocks can occur. If the need arises to put a green thread to sleep, usually the entire OS thread below it has to go to sleep as well.

Sun HotSpot uses native threads. Native threads use the operating system's native ability to manage multithreaded processes; in particular, they use the `pthread` library. When you run native threads, the kernel schedules and manages the various threads that make up the process. Sun HotSpot relies completely on whatever threads a particular OS offers. On Solaris they are lightweight processes (LWPs), on Linux they are just first-class processes. So, if you run a multithreaded Java app and execute `ps`, you see a whole lot of processes for just a single JVM. The newer kernels are different in listing the threads as processes and put them as an entry in `/proc` filesystem. On Windows, they are windows threads. So context switching is performed naturally, by the OS.

Native threads create the appearance that many Java processes are running, and each thread takes up its own entry in the process table. One clue that these are all threads of the same process is that the memory size is identical for all the threads — they are all using the same memory.

Green threads emulate multithreaded environments without relying on any native OS capabilities. They run code in user space that manages and schedules threads; Sun wrote green threads to enable Java to work in environments that do not have native thread support.

On multi-CPU machines, native threads can run more than one thread simultaneously by assigning different threads to different CPUs. Green threads run on only one CPU.

Oracle WebLogic offers two JVMs

Oracle WebLogic ships two JVMs in its product—Sun HotSpot and BEA JRockit. As you can see in the following screenshot, during installation you can choose which JVM you want to use.

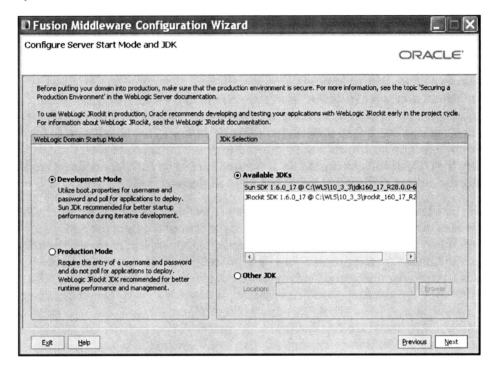

Sun's HotSpot versus JRockit

It perhaps sounds a bit strange to choose between two different products practically serving the same purpose.

In 2008 and 2009, Oracle made some large acquisitions, that resulted in taking over two big companies, BEA and later on Sun. Both developed their own JVM, and to this day Oracle still hasn't merged the two products into one, so you are still able to choose between them.

As of the time of writing this book, the merge still hasn't taken place, but it probably will occur somewhere in mid 2012.

Sun JDK uses interpreter (Interpreter and JIT in previous releases)

In this mechanism, the bytecode is read and then translated into machine language, but these results are not saved in the memory. So even if the same method is run again and again, the JVM has to translate the code into machine language every time. This means that the machine code will not be reusable as it is not saved anywhere in the memory.

Oracle JRockit uses only JIT compiler (Just In Time)

JIT mechanism means, once a method is run, that the bytecode is translated to machine language and this is saved in the memory. This means that if the method is run again, there is no need for translation and the machine code is reused.

Because of the interpreter mechanism used by the Sun JDK, the startup time for the server is faster because it does not have to save the machine code in memory. Once the translation is done for a method, it moves to the other one. However, Oracle JRockit saves the code, hence starting up takes longer. For the same reason, Oracle JRockit uses more memory than Sun JVM.

In the long run, JRockit gives a slightly better performance as compared to Sun. Oracle JRockit optimizes the code. It identifies the HOT SPOTS, that is, the methods that are being run more often. These methods are then queued up for optimization. This code is then optimized, which improves performance. Many issues arise because of the code optimization mechanism as it is a complex procedure. Optimization can be disabled.

JIT is also used by Sun JDK, but that was in the earlier versions. The Java HotSpot VM removes the need for a JIT compiler in most cases.

Memory spaces

The JVM memory consists of the following segments:

* Heap Memory, which is the storage for Java objects.
* Non-Heap Memory, which is used by Java to store loaded classes and other metadata.
* JVM code itself, JVM internal structures, loaded profiler agent code, data, and so on.

What are memory spaces? Memory is managed in generations, or memory pools holding objects of different ages. Garbage collection occurs in each generation when the generation fills up. Objects are allocated in a generation for younger objects, or for the young generation, and because of infant mortality most objects die there.

Sun JDK has the following memory spaces: Eden space, survivor space, tenured generation, and permanent generation. The objects move from one space to another according to their age and survival from garbage collection.

JRockit has two spaces: young generation and old generation. It uses the same mechanism of garbage collection. JRockit doesn't have a permanent generation.

Memory and other JVM tunings

JRockit provides advanced JVM tunings. After the release of R26, JRockit now takes care of a few of the tunings by itself. For example, if there is an "out of memory" occurring on the native TLA in previous releases due to insufficient TLA size—which is 2k by default—in the later releases JRockit tunes these settings as per the requirement of the application.

The TLA or Thread Local Area is some free space reserved in the JVM and dedicated to a thread for its exclusive use. A thread can allocate small objects in its own TLA without synchronizing with other threads.

Perhaps these terms sound a bit confusing for you, but if you become a more experienced administrator, it's good to know where the differences lie between the two JVMs.

Oracle recommends using the Sun JVM in development mode and JRockit in production mode.

JRockit was always built more for server environments, while Sun's HotSpot was more focused on client side JVMs. The result was that JRockit always had a better overall performance and some more advanced diagnostic tools.

Today, the difference between them has decreased and choosing Sun JVM is almost as good as choosing JRockit. For now, tooling is a major differentiator between the two.

JVM crashes

When JRockit crashes, a JRockit dump is produced, which basically has the reason for the crash. JRockit uses native libraries by default. Native libraries are libraries outside the Java code, and used by the OS or other programs as well. This can be disabled by disabling the Native IO from the Admin console. The most common reason for the JRockit crash is the conflict between native libraries, for example the jdbc type 2 drivers which use native libs. It is recommended to use type 4 pure Java drivers when using Oracle JRockit. The stack trace in the JRockit dump will show the exact cause. When the JVM crashes, it is important to test it again by disabling code optimization and checking if the issue still persists.

A Sun JVM crash produces a `hs_err_pid` file, which has the root cause of the crash. There can be several reasons for a Sun JVM crash, such as some bugs (defects in the code of the JVM). These issues need to be reported to the Sun team.

Tools for performance tracking

Sun JDK that comes bundled with WebLogic Server provides tools such as JConsole, which can be used for performance tracking and monitoring the memory in use, by the JVM. This tool is very helpful to determine each and every detail about the memory being used by the application, CPU usage, and memory leaks.

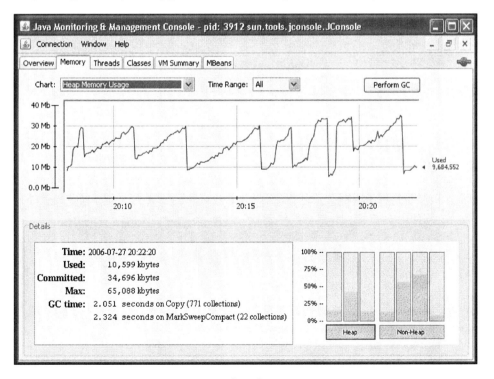

Oracle JRockit has a much more advanced tool, JRMC (JRockit Mission Control), which provides advanced tracking features. JRA recordings can be taken, that give every detail about the JVM arguments, garbage collection details, methods using the maximum memory, and so on. The memory leak detector tool in JRMC is also another important and very helpful tool. These features make it easy for the user and administrators to maintain a record and identify the issues with the application and the JVM.

The JVM in relation to Oracle WebLogic Server

In the previous section, we took a closer look at the JVMs that could be used within Oracle WebLogic. But where can we position the JVM?

In fact, every WebLogic Server instance is a running JVM. Every Admin Server in any domain executes within a JVM. The same also counts for Managed Servers as explained in *Chapter 5, Managed Servers and the Node Manager*.

JVM startup commands

The following diagram gives a schematic overview of a running JVM. Note the different memory options that you can add to the start parameters of the JVM.

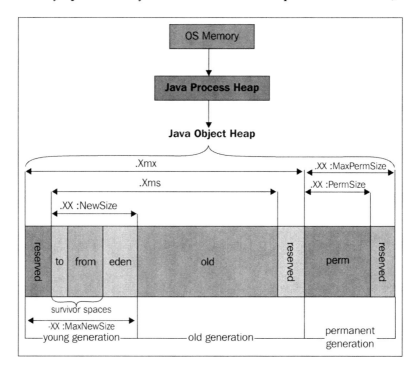

The previous diagram shows an overview of the configured MaxSize (Xmx) spanning the entire JVM. The initial memory size (Xms) is configured to a lower value. The terms in the previous diagram are explained as follows:

- **Young generation space**: It is meant for recently created objects.

- **Eden space (heap)**: It is the pool from which memory is initially allocated for most objects. It is part a of the young generation.

- **Permanent generation (non-heap)**: It is the pool that contains all the reflective data of the virtual machine itself, such as the class and method objects. With Java VMs that use class data sharing, this generation is divided into read-only and read-write areas.

- **Old generation space**: This stores surviving objects that have lived to some extent.

If objects get too old, or young generation space gets filled up, JVM promotes objects to the old generation space. When the old generation space gets filled up, the JVM performs a major collection to remove the unused objects and reclaim their space. A major *GarbageCollect* takes a significant amount of time and can affect system performance.

Configure your JVMs for WebLogic

When you create a Managed Server, it takes its initial startup parameters from the setDomainEnv.sh/cmd file, which resides in the <DOMAIN_HOME/bin directory.

By default two parameters are set:

- Xms: The initial heapsize
- Xmx: The max heapsize

A good practice for many applications is to set equal initial and max heapsize.

When you set -Xms1G -Xmx2G, the committed heap (that is the physical heap that we will actually use) starts at 1G. This means that there are pages of memory that contain the state of the 1G heap. Whether those pages are physically on RAM or are in swap is something that the JVM does not explicitly control. It's something that the OS controls, and it depends on the *environment* (memory pressure) and the state of the host, so it could reserve the remaining for other tasks. In this case, it is an advantage if the JVM claims the entire RAM at once.

In short, setting -Xms does what it says on the box, that is, it sets the initial memory pool sizes to the value. After that, Java just resumes its normal behavior of allocating memory. This is shown in the next screenshot:

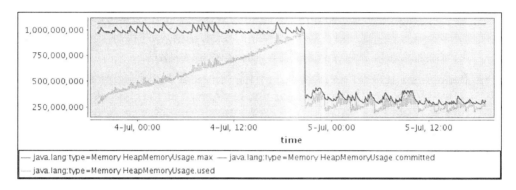

As you can see in the previous screenshot, when you specify -Xms to be the same as -Xmx, the blue line immediately starts out at the maximum level. It stays up there for a while, but after that the blue line drops sharply. From then on, Java does what it always does—it allocates and de-allocates memory from the operating system. This behavior seems to be controlled from the PS MarkSweep garbage collector. Java leaves the committed memory (relatively) untouched, until a full GC is performed. The first full *GarbageCollect* coincides with the sharp drop in committed memory. In the full GC, it ignores the -Xms setting and returns a large portion of the feed.

Setting the JVM HeapSize

There are four options to set your Managed Server JVM options:

- Through the Admin console, in the **Server Start** tab
- In the startManagedWeblogic script
- In the SetDomainEnv script
- In the java Weblogic.Server command

Setting the JVM through the Admin console

When you click on the **Servers** tab, click on the Managed Server of your choice, and select the **Server Start** tab. In the **options** field, you can set any parameter that your Managed Server requires.

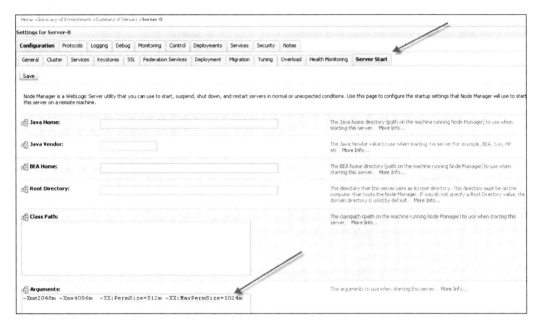

Setting the JVM in the startManagedWeblogic script

If you want to use the startup script to start your Managed Servers, then try to update the Managed Server script `startManagedWebLogic.sh/cmd`, which is under the `<MW_HOME>/user_projects/domains/<DOMAIN_NAME>/bin` directory, with the required heap size in `JAVA_OPTIONS` parameter.

For example:

```
JAVA_OPTIONS="-Xms2g -Xmx2g" ${JAVA_OPTIONS}
```

Setting the JVM in the setDomainEnv script

If you want to set it domain-wide, you can edit the `setDomainEnv.sh/cmd` script, which is also under the `<MW_HOME>/user_projects/domains/<DOMAIN_NAME>/bin` directory.

```
if [ "${SERVER_NAME}" = "AdminServer" ] ; then    USER_MEM_ARGS="..."
  export USER_MEM_ARGS
fi
```

```
if [ "${SERVER_NAME}" = "managed_server1" ] ; then
  USER_MEM_ARGS="..."
  export USER_MEM_ARGS
fi
```

Setting the JVM in the Java Weblogic.Server startup command

If you would like to use Java `WebLogic.Server` to startup, you can use something similar to the following code:

```
java -Xms256m -Xmx512m -Dweblogic.Name=SimpleManagedServer -Dweblogic.
management.server=http://localhost:7001 -Dweblogic.RootDirectory=
c:\my_domains\SimpleDomain weblogic.Server
```

Some optional JVM arguments

Sometimes only setting the `Xms` and `Xmx` arguments are not sufficient enough, so here are some additional arguments you can think of:

Basic Sun JVM arguments

- `-Xms`: The initial amount of heap allocated to the JVM
- `-Xmx`: The maximum amount of heap that this JVM can allocate
- `-XX:NewSize` (default 2 MB): Default size of new generation (in bytes)
- `-XX:MaxNewSize`: Maximum size of new generation (in bytes). Since 1.4, MaxNewSize is computed as a function of NewRatio
- `-XX:NewRatio` (default = 2): Ratio of new to old generation sizes
- `-XX:SurvivorRatio` (default = 8): Ratio of Eden size to one survivor space size
- `-XX:TargetSurvivorRatio` (default = 50%): Desired percentage of survivor space used after cleaning up
- `-XX:MaxPermSize`: Maximum size of the permanent generation

Basic JRockit JVM arguments

- `-Xms`: The initial amount of heap allocated to the JVM.
- `-Xmx`: The maximum amount of heap that this JVM can allocate.

- -Xns: Size of the nursery generation in the heap. The nursery is an area of the heap where new objects are allocated. When the nursery becomes full it is garbage collected separately in a young collection.

- -XgcPrio: A priority level that helps to determine which GC algorithms the JVM will use at runtime(This option is also available in Sun JVM from Java 5).

- throughput: Maximize application throughout.

- pausetime: Minimize the length of Garbage Collect intervals.

- deterministic: Consistent response times.

- -XXcompactRatio: The percentage of the heap.

Common JVM issues

Although you're an excellent administrator and configurator, there are still issues that you might not have thought of yet, that could occur with your JVM. So let's discuss some of the common issues you could encounter:

Out of memory

JVMs trigger java.lang.OutOfMemoryError when there is insufficient memory to perform some task. An out of memory condition can occur when there is free memory available in the heap but it is too fragmented and not contiguously located to store the object being allocated or moved (as part of a garbage collection cycle).

Memory leak

A common cause of memory leak errors is excessive caching. JVMs trigger java.lang.OutOfMemoryError when there is insufficient memory to perform some task. An out-of-memory condition can occur when there is free memory available in the heap but it is too fragmented and not contiguously located to store the object being allocated or moved (as part of a garbage collection cycle).

JVM crash

You can identify and troubleshoot a JVM crash by the diagnostic files that are generated by the JVM. A snapshot is created that captures that state of the JVM process at the time of the error.

This binary file contains information about the entire JVM process and needs to be opened using debugging tools. The *gdb* debugging tool, popular on Linux, can extract useful information from core files. You can try attaching to the JVM process with GDB (gdb - [process id]) and get a backtrace (bt). You might be able to figure out where in your program the problem lies, from the current native code execution. To find the process, you execute: ps -ef | grep java.

The following screenshot shows the output from GDB:

```
(gdb) dump_inlinetree 0x8915640
0x8915640:      Test.previousSpaceIndex
0x8915930:          java/io/PrintStream.print
0x8915a48:              java/io/PrintStream.write
0x8915d30:                  java/io/PrintStream.ensureOpen
---Type <return> to continue, or q <return> to quit---
0x8915e28:                  java/io/Writer.write
0x8915ea0:                      java/lang/String.length
0x8915f18:                  java/io/BufferedWriter.write
0x8916240:                      java/io/BufferedWriter.ensureOpen
---Type <return> to continue, or q <return> to quit---
0x8916348:                  java/io/BufferedWriter.min
0x8916440:                      java/lang/String.getChars
0x8916728:                  java/io/BufferedWriter.flushBuffer
0x8916998:                      java/io/BufferedWriter.ensureOpen
---Type <return> to continue, or q <return> to quit---
0x8916b08:              java/io/BufferedWriter.flushBuffer
0x8916d40:                  java/io/BufferedWriter.ensureOpen
0x8916e38:          java/io/OutputStreamWriter.flushBuffer
```

On the Sun JVM, the logfile is named hs_err_pid<pid>.log, where <pid> is the process ID of the process. JRockit refers to this error log as a *dump* file, and is named JRockit.<pid>.dump.

Basic JVM Tools

- **Java Stack Trace**: A Java stack trace is a snapshot of the threads and monitors in a JVM. A stack trace can have thousands of lines of diagnostics.

- **Thread Dump:** You can generate a partial Java stack trace, which in this case is only the thread's information, by using the `Thread.dumpStack` method, or the `printStackTrace` method. Use the kill `-3` option to kill the JVM process.

- **Verbose GC:** Add `-verbosegc -XX:+PrintGCDetails` to indicate a problem with garbage collection.

Sun JVM diagnostic tools

JRockit Mission Control has the following tools:

- **JVisualVM**: It is the graphical interface for monitoring performance.

The next screenshot shows the output screen:

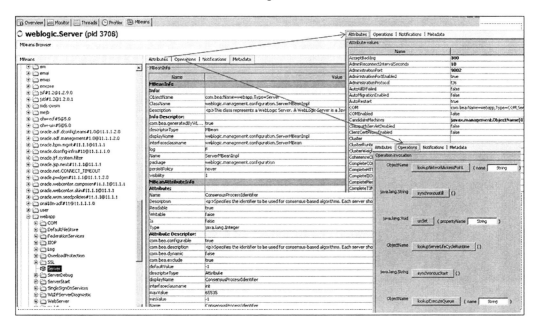

- **JConsole**: It is the lightweight version of JVisualVM.

  You can connect to WebLogic Server's MBeans through JConsole.

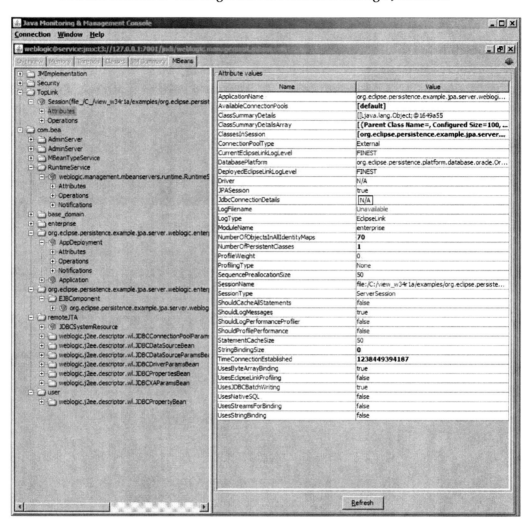

JRockit diagnostic tools

JRockit Mission Control has the following tools:

- **The JRockit Management Console:** This console can be used to analyze and monitor running instances of JRockit. It provides real-time information about the running applications.

The following screenshot shows the Mission Control Console.

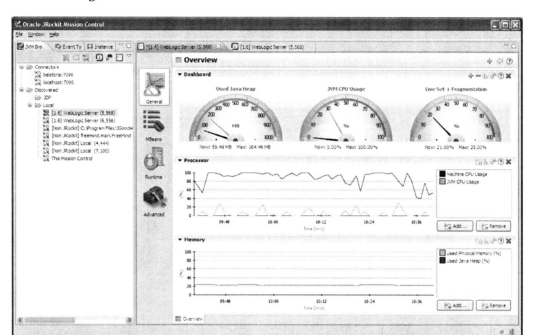

- **The JRockit Runtime Analyzer (JRA):** This is built into the JRockit JVM. The tool collects data as your application runs, giving you information that is within the JVM itself.

- **The JRockit Memory Leak Detector (Memleak):** This can be executed from the Management Console.

The following screenshot shows the memory leak detector; you can enable it by clicking the **MemLeakDetector** button, and the detector will spot for memory that has not been released.

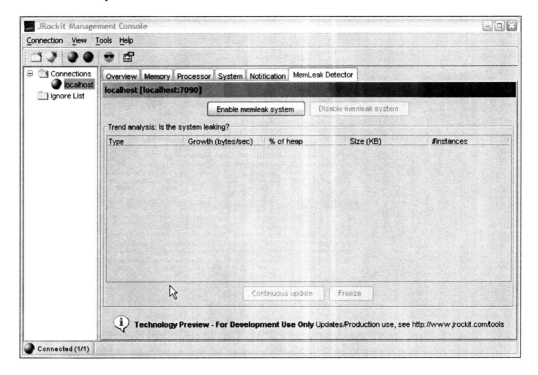

Summary

There are many topics we could include about this subject, but then we would run out of ink and paper discussing them all in depth.

For modern platforms such as WebLogic, the JVM is—as you have seen in this chapter—an important component, and requires a good level of knowledge about how applications deal with the JVM.

There are several ways to detect failures in your WebLogic Server environment and troubles with your JVM. So in the next chapter, you will learn to be a proactive troubleshooter.

10

What if Something Goes Wrong?

The title of this chapter seems a bit frightening, but don't worry, Oracle WebLogic Server usually deals with common problems in a good way. The platform is robust and solid.

But sometimes there are some unforeseen issues. Although you configured all bits and pieces very well, external causes can make your system unstable.

Or perhaps you could make a tiny mistake or misjudgment, which can lead to some problems in your WebLogic Server.

This is where your analytical and troubleshooting skills come in, along with your great deal of experience.

This chapter will give you a start in the areas you could begin to troubleshoot. Although there are many possible scenarios, in real life often the same issues will appear and can be easily tackled.

Diagnostic patterns

In case of a failure or other problems in your WebLogic Server, it is good to follow a structured way to detect and diagnose any problem.

Following diagnostic patterns can help you to solve your problems in a quick and effective way.

Server core dump pattern

An application creates a core dump file when a WebLogic Server process terminates due to some invalid native code (machine-specific code). A server crash, JVM crash, machine crash, or HotSpot error may also be associated with this occurrence. This pattern will describe what steps are needed to gather information from a core file on various platforms.

In order to determine the cause of a WebLogic Server crash, you need to determine all potential sources of native code used by the WebLogic Server process. The places to focus on are:

- **The WebLogic Server performance pack**. Major performance improvements are witnessed when you use native performance packs on machines that host WebLogic Server instances. The WebLogic Server performance pack is a native code and when enabled could potentially produce such an error. Disable this feature to determine if that is the cause. You can do this via the console or via the command line. Using the console, look under the Server tab by setting **NativeIOEnabled** to `false`. See the section **Enabling Performance Packs** to get the exact sequence of steps under the **Server** tab in the console. The steps are:
    - Access the Administration Console for the domain.
    - Expand the Servers node in the left pane to display the servers configured in your domain.
    - Click the name of the server instance that you want to configure.
    - Select the **Configuration | Tuning** tab.
    - If the **Enable Native IO** checkbox is selected, please deselect it so that it is *not* enabled now.
    - Click **Apply**.
    - Restart the server.

  You can also do this via the Java options to the start command for WebLogic Server. Set `-Dweblogic.NativeIOEnabled=false` on the command line and then start the server. The command line will take precedence over what is sent via the console. When we will be certain that the Native I/O is causing it, only then it is recommended to disable it.

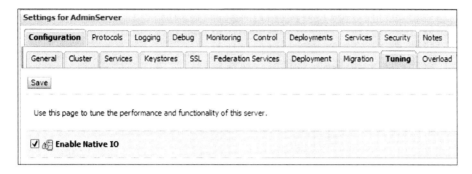

- Any earlier Type JDBC driver, such as ODBC, makes use of native DBMS libraries, which could also produce errors. It depends on native libraries of the underlying operating system the JVM is running on. Also, use of this driver leads to other installation dependencies; for example, ODBC must be installed on the computer having the driver and the database must support an ODBC driver. Use a pure Java Oracle or other JDBC driver in order to determine if that is the cause. This you can set under the JDBC service, which could be the cause of the problem.

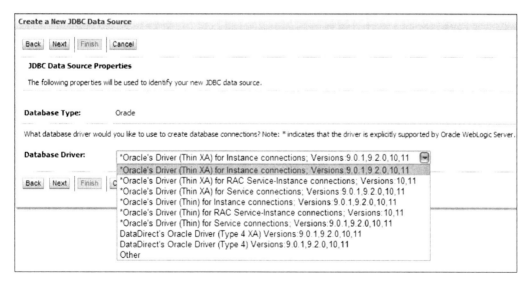

- The JVM itself is a native program and can cause such errors. When in doubt, try another certified JVM and/or a later release to determine if a JVM bug is at fault. Many JVM bugs involve the use of the JIT compiler and disabling this feature will often resolve this type of problem. Usually this can be done by supplying the `-Djava.compiler=none` command option.

- Sometimes the JVM will produce a small log file that may contain useful information. The file is produced in the directory where WebLogic Server was started and it is of the format `hs_err_pid.log`, where PID is the Process ID of the WebLogic Server process.

The following block of code is a sample of an `hs_err_pid.log`:

```
hs_err_pidXXXX.log
--------------------------------------------------
#
# A fatal error has been detected by the Java Runtime Environment:
#
# SIGSEGV (0xb) at pc=0xb7116982, pid=15011, tid=1672133520
#
# JRE version: 6.0_18-b07
# Java VM: Java HotSpot(TM) Server VM (16.0-b13 mixed mode linux-x86 )
# Problematic frame:
# V [libjvm.so+0x495982]
#
# If you would like to submit a bug report, please visit:
# http://java.sun.com/webapps/bugreport/crash.jsp
#


--------------- T H R E A D ----------------

Current thread (0x08ddb400): JavaThread
"SocketAcceptorIoProcessor-1.2" [_thread_in_vm, id=15329,
stack(0x63a5b000,0x63aac000)]

siginfo:si_signo=SIGSEGV: si_errno=0, si_code=1 (SEGV_MAPERR), si_
addr=0xff654e8d

Registers:
EAX=0xb73ca50c, EBX=0xb73d8de0, ECX=0x68d1b310, EDX=0x63aaaad0
ESP=0x63aaaa50, EBP=0x63aaaa58, ESI=0xff654e89, EDI=0x9aea1dc1
EIP=0xb7116982, CR2=0xff654e8d, EFLAGS=0x00010286

Top of Stack: (sp=0x63aaaa50)
0x63aaaa50: b73d8de0 08ddb400 63aaab08 b7297262
0x63aaaa60: ff654e89 08ddb400 00000000 00000000
0x63aaaa70: 9ab13138 0805c8d0 63aaaac8 e0000000
0x63aaaa80: 0805c8d0 9ab13138 63aaaa98 9aea1dd1
0x63aaaa90: 00000008 9ab13138 63aaaac8 00000001
0x63aaaaa0: 9aea1dc3 08b210ac 63aaaad0 9aea1e05
0x63aaaab0: 9addf030 00000001 08b210ac 08b210ac
0x63aaaac0: b73d0608 08ddb400 63aaac48 b723d17e
```

```
Instructions:  (pc=0xb7116982)
0xb7116972:  75 08 8b 83 f8 21 00 00 3b 30 0f 84 a4 00 00 00
0xb7116982:  8b 46 04 83 ec 0c 8d 48 08 8b 40 08 51 ff 90 8c

Stack:  [0x63a5b000,0x63aac000], sp=0x63aaaa50, free space=13e63aaa3e0k
Native frames:  (J=compiled Java code, j=interpreted, Vv=VM code,
C=native code)
V  [libjvm.so+0x495982]
V  [libjvm.so+0x616262]
V  [libjvm.so+0x61408a]
V  [libjvm.so+0x613f67]
V  [libjvm.so+0x5c92ce]
```

Gathering core dump data for Linux

GDB is the default preferred Linux debugger and it is powerful and stable. There are also various visual debuggers available, but only a simple command-line debugger is really needed to get the stack trace from the core. GDB lets you see the internal structure of a program, print out variable values, set breakpoints, and runs in a single step through source code. It makes an extremely powerful tool for fixing problems in the program code.

Run `<file_name> /core` to verify if the core file is from the Java VM.

Make sure you are using the latest GDB version from GNU on Linux to avoid any known bugs. See: `http://ftp.gnu.org/gnu/gdb/`.

Also make sure that the `ulimit` for a core file is set on Linux (for example, `ulimit -c unlimited`).

On Linux, the core dump is turned off by default on all systems. In most Linux versions, it should be under the `/etc/security` directory. There should be a file called `limits.conf`. The file itself is self-explanatory. Look for the word "core", if set to `0`, then core dump is disabled.

Get a stack trace using GDB, as follows (same as done previously, see *JVM Crash* section from *Chapter 9, The Heart of Oracle WebLogic Server: The JVM*):

```
$ java -version (need to use right version of jdk)
$ ls /usr/local/bin/gdb (need to know gdb location) or "which gdb"
$ export DEBUG_PROG=/usr/local/bin/gdb (or wherever "gdb" is located)
$ gdb /java corefile
```

Now you will be in the debugger. Execute the following commands:

```
(gdb) where ("shows a summary of the stack")
(gdb) thr ("switch among threads or show the current thread")
(gdb) info thr ("inquire about existing threads")
(gdb) thread apply 1 bt ("apply a command to a list of threads,
  specifically the backtrace to thread #1")
(gdb) quit
```

Using these commands will produce a stack trace of the last thread that was executed (`wherethr` command), show the state of all the threads (`info thrthread apply 1 bt` command).

Using the last command (`thread apply # bt`) is a way to get the stack trace of an individual thread by replacing # with an actual thread number or you can replace # with `all` to get the stack trace for all the threads.

If your OS has none of these tools, you can use `pmap` and `pstack` to analyze a core dump. For example: `/usr/proc/bin/pstack coredumpfile`.

You also can use strings command and filter on errors in the dump file.

Core files from a Sun's JVM JIT Compiler

You could investigate the JVM Core Dump with the Linux `pstack` command. The output would be something similar to the following:

```
fe16d550 __1cMURShiftINodeFValue6kMpnOPhaseTransform__pknEType__ (9983c8,
88d00d4c, 1, 0, fe570000, 3b7480) + f8
fe0d2180 __1cMPhaseIterGVNNtransform_old6MpnENode__2_ (88d00d4c, 3b795c,
9c, 88d00e9c, 11, e4c4d8) + 1d4
fe19b1e8 __1cMPhaseIterGVNIoptimize6M_v_ (88d00d4c, 0, fe5b89f8, 0, 0, 0)
+ a0
fe202008 __1cHCompileIOptimize6M_v_ (88d01298, fe5335c4, 88d011ac,
fe570000, 0, 0) + 168
fe2008b4 __1cHCompile2t6MpnFciEnv_pnHciScope_pnIciMethod_iii_v_
(fe5333f9, 371584, 2f1d24, d30664, ffffffff, 1) + bac
fe1fd08c __1cKC2CompilerOcompile_method6MpnFciEnv_pnHciScope_pnIciMethod_
ii_v_ (2bb80, 88d01ab4, 0, 372918, ffffffff, 0) + 64
fe1fc850 __1cNCompileBrokerZinvoke_compiler_on_method6FpnLCompileTask__v_
(720, 0, ffffffff, fe5aee50, fe5bbbe4, eaff8) + 61c
fe2ac1f8 __1cNCompileBrokerUcompiler_thread_loop6F_v_ (fe533c01,
fe5af218, eaff8, eb5a8, 306d10, fe269254) + 428
fe26927c __1cKJavaThreadDrun6M_v_ (eaff8, b, 40, 0, a, ff37c000) + 284
fe26575c _start (eaff8, ff37d658, 1, 1, ff37c000, 0) + 134
ff36b01c _thread_start (eaff8, 0, 0, 0, 0, 0) + 40
```

In order to determine which method caused this, add the following flags to the Java server line and run your test again to make the server core dump to obtain information:

```
-XX:+PrintCompilation -XX:+PrintOpto
```

This can be set in your `startWebLogic` script or your `setDomainEnv` script.

With the output from `PrintCompilation`, you could filter which method is failing and ask the developer to filter this out of the code.

Some output after enabling this option:

```
BenchmarkLoopTest emptyLoop 1000000 3 3
   1        java.lang.String::hashCode (60 bytes)
   2        java.lang.String::charAt (33 bytes)
   3        java.lang.String::indexOf (166 bytes)
Are you ready?
y

Waking up the JIT compiler...
   4        java.lang.String::indexOf (151 bytes)
Run: 1, Time: 6146, Test returns: 3
Run: 2, Time: 3353, Test returns: 3
Run: 3, Time: 3353, Test returns: 3
...
Run: 15, Time: 3632, Test returns: 3
   5        sun.reflect.ClassFileAssembler::emitByte (11 bytes)
   6        sun.reflect.ByteVectorImpl::add (38 bytes)
Run: 16, Time: 3632, Test returns: 3
...
Run: 37, Time: 3353, Test returns: 3
   7   !    sun.nio.cs.SingleByteEncoder::encodeArrayLoop (475 bytes)
Run: 38, Time: 3352, Test returns: 3
...
Run: 96, Time: 3352, Test returns: 3
   8        sun.nio.cs.Surrogate::is (18 bytes)
Run: 97, Time: 3353, Test returns: 3
Run: 98, Time: 4749, Test returns: 3
   9        java.lang.Object::<iRun: nit> (1 bytes)
99, Time: 3352, Test returns: 3
---   n    java.lang.System::arraycopy (static)
Run: 100, Time: 3352, Test returns: 3
...
```

```
Run: 221, Time: 3073, Test returns: 3
  10       java.lang.String::getChars (66 bytes)
Run: 222, Time: 3073, Test returns: 3
...
... Some other methods compiled
```

Generic Server Hang Pattern

The next pattern in which you could search for crashes is the Generic Server Hang Pattern.

WebLogic Server can hang because of various reasons, but the most important ones are:

- Extensively high load
- Threads that are hanging
- Other resources such as JDBC, JMS cause the server to hang
- Badly programmed applications

A server hang is suspected when the server does not respond to new requests, requests time out, or requests take longer to process.

In fact, every component can cause the WebLogic Server to hang if it's consuming extensively more resources than it was planned to be.

Hanging can have internal causes such as spinning processes- these are eating 100 percent CPU and you can't kill it even with kill-9- or external failures of network, load balancers, databases, or other systems to connect to.

The following table shows some well-known causes of a generic server hang. Let's have a look at some of them:

Pattern Name	Topic
EJB_RMI Server Hang	RMI, RJVM responses — all threads tied up waiting for RJVM, RMI responses.
Application Deadlock Causes Server Hang	Application Deadlock — thread locks resource1 then waits for lock for resource2. Another thread locks resource2 and then waits for lock for resource1.
Thread Usage Server Hang	Threads are all used up, none available for new work.
Garbage Collection Server Hang	Garbage Collection taking too much time.

Pattern Name	Topic
JSP cause Server Hang	JSP improper settings for servlet times, for example, PageCheckSeconds.
JDBC Causes Server Hang	Long Running JDBC calls or JDBC deadlocks lead to a hang.
Server Hang in Code Optimization	JVM hang during (code optimization), looks like server hang.
JSP Compilation Server Hang	JSP compilation causes server hang under heavy load.

EJB_RMI Server Hang

What causes in general an EJB/Application to hang?

This problem occurs because of a poor design due to lack of knowledge about how clustered objects are stored and retrieved from the WebLogic JNDI tree when clustered. This results in waiting calls.

The threads associated with an EJB_RMI Server Hang have a typical pattern, as shown next. If many "default" queue threads in the thread dump have the same stack trace, chances are that the hang problem is related to using remote JNDI lookups.

Unnecessary network traffic is causing threads to wait for responses to outstanding rmi/rjvm requests in clustered EJB applications. These requests are a result of remote JNDI lookups in a clustered domain.

The following is an example of an application with problems:

```
"ExecuteThread: '52' for queue: 'default'" daemon prio=5
tid=0x4b3e40b0 nid=0x1170 waiting on monitor [0x4c74f000..0x4c74fdbc]
at java.lang.Object.wait(Native Method)
at WebLogic.rjvm.ResponseImpl.waitForData(ResponseImpl.java:72)
at WebLogic.rjvm.ResponseImpl.getTxContext(ResponseImpl.java:97)
at WebLogic.rmi.internal.BasicOutboundRequest.sendReceive(BasicOutboun
dRequest.java:80)
at WebLogic.rmi.cluster.ReplicaAwareRemoteRef.
invoke(ReplicaAwareRemoteRef.java:262)
at WebLogic.rmi.cluster.ReplicaAwareRemoteRef.
invoke(ReplicaAwareRemoteRef.java:229)
at WebLogic.rmi.internal.ProxyStub.invoke(ProxyStub.java:35)
at $Proxy6.lookup(Unknown Source)
at WebLogic.jndi.internal.WLContextImpl.lookup(WLContextImpl.java:341)
```

In the stack trace of this thread, you see some issues already. The thread is in a wait method and is therefore waiting for something to occur, that is, work or data to arrive.

It called this `wait()` because it is waiting for data from a remote JVM in the method `WebLogic.rjvm.ResponseImpl.waitForData()`.

If many threads in the stack are waiting for data from other cluster members, the other cluster members are probably waiting for data from this JVM. In this case, it's an EJB application which has problems with clustering features of WebLogic. Investigate if CLASSPATHs on different hosts are equal; ask your developer if EJBs are clusterable, or else deploy them as pinned services. It also could be a Classloader issue. Use a tool such as `wls-cat` to investigate class loading.

ServerHang—application deadlock

An inadvertent deadlock in the application code can cause a server to hang. For example, a situation in which thread1 is waiting for resource1 and is holding a lock on resource2, while thread2 needs resource2 and is holding the lock on resource1. Neither thread can progress.

Deadly embrace: One of the deadlock problems is the deadly embrace: Thread1 owns lock A and waits on lock B, thread2 owns lock B and waits on lock A. These threads are deadlocked and will remain blocked in this state. In many cases, the remaining threads will eventually enter the deadlock by attempting to acquire lock A or lock B and waiting. For instance, you might have a servlet that calls a synchronized method on the B object. If B's monitor is already held in a deadlock, any subsequent servlet request that attempts to acquire that monitor will enter the deadlock.

Taking a thread dump is the best practice to discover a deadly embrace deadlock. Most virtual machines include a thread state for each Java thread in the dump.

The most common thread states are:

- R – running
- MW – monitor wait
- CW – condition wait

The following screenshot shows an application in the CW state:

```
"ExecuteThread: '16' for queue: 'weblogic.kernel.Default'" daemon prio=5 tid=0x010dc720 nid=0x29 in Object.wait()
[a1a7f000..a1a7fc30]
at java.lang.Object.wait(Native Method)
at java.lang.Object.wait(Object.java:429)
at weblogic.kernel.ExecuteThread.waitForRequest(ExecuteThread.java:154) - locked <0xb1593fa0> (a
weblogic.kernel.ExecuteThread)
at weblogic.kernel.ExecuteThread.run(ExecuteThread.java:174)
```

Threads in the MW state are blocked, waiting to enter a synchronized block and acquire a Java monitor. Since the thread dump includes the Java thread's stack trace, it's also possible to determine which monitor is blocking the thread. If multiple threads are in the MW state on the same monitor, it's a good indication that there's either a lot of contention for this monitor, or the server is deadlocked. In a deadlock situation, you should be able to determine the other threads blocked in MW and their held monitors.

There are two approaches for solving deadly embrace deadlocks: deadlock avoidance and deadlock detection. Deadlock avoidance is more of a developer's method by structuring the code, so that it can't hit the deadlock case. A common solution is to implement lock ordering.

In deadlock detection, deadlocks are automatically discovered and one or more deadlocks are killed and release their locks to break the deadlock. Java virtual machines do not break deadlocks on Java monitors, so deadlock avoidance is necessary. Using tools like JConsole or JRockit Runtime Analyzer can detect and monitor deadlocks.

Out-of-threads deadlock: Another type of deadlock is the "out of threads" deadlock. This deadlock often doesn't show up until a load test or, in the worst case, when your production application receives a lot of traffic. In this scenario, your WebLogic Server is running with a fixed number of threads. The application includes logic where a given request or action performs work in one thread and then blocks on work that must be done in another thread.

The best way to avoid "out of threads" deadlocks is to analyze your architecture and remove the common mistakes that produce these deadlocks. For example, never open a socket connection to your own server instance. For best socket performance, you use the native socket reader implementation rather than the Java implementation, on machines that host WebLogic Server instances. However, if you must use the pure-Java socket reader implementation for host machines, you can still improve the performance of socket communication by configuring the proper number of execute threads to act as socket reader threads for each server instance and client machine.

When you don't use Native IO, fill in the percentage of Socket Readers in the tuning tab of the server instance.

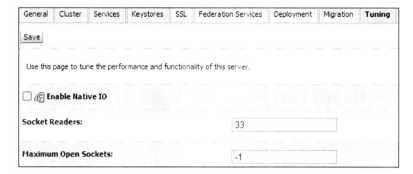

Also, avoid synchronous request/response APIs that include callbacks. Generally, asynchronous communication works well for server-to-server or application-to-application calls. Both messaging (JMS) and Web services include asynchronous support. One of the advantages of asynchronous communication is that the calling thread is not blocked waiting for the response.

Also a good practice is using work managers. Incoming requests are assigned an internal priority based on the configuration of work managers you create to manage the work performed by your applications. With work managers, WebLogic Server can prioritize work and allocate the threads based on an execution model. This is taken care of by the administrator-defined parameters after observing the actual runtime performance, throughput, monitoring, and so on. Defining of this behavior or rules is done at different levels for different applications or group of applications. You can have a default work manager, which is used to handle thread management and perform self-tuning. This work manager is used by an application if no other work managers are specified in the application's deployment descriptors.

In many situations, the default Work Manager may be sufficient for most application requirements. WebLogic Server's thread-handling algorithms assign each application its own fair share by default.

Global Work Managers have the scope of the domain. You can create them in the WebLogic Administration Console:

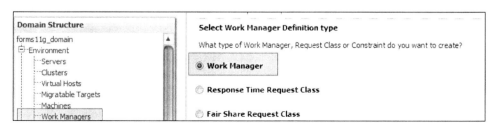

JDBC server hang pattern

There can be different possible reasons for JDBC calls to lead to a hanging WLS instance, such as use of `DriverManager.getConnection()` in JDBC code, long running SQL queries, hanging database, slow network, application-level deadlock, problems with RefreshMinutes or TestFrequencySeconds settings, and pool shrinking. JDBC connection pool shrinking and re-creation of database connections causes long response times.

This pattern addresses troubleshooting for these common problems. See the JDBC resource at the **Pool** tab, **Diagnostics**. You could enable options to get deeper into analysis.

To get behind JDBC problems you can enable some debug options in WebLogic Server, such as:

- jDriver JDBC tracing can be switched on via the administration console, or in the `config.xml` file directly by setting `<JDBCLoggingEnabled>` in the Server tag.

- The `ServerDebugMBean` has some JDBC-related flags that can be turned on in the `config.xml` file. Please put a new `<ServerDebug>` tag into the `<Server>` tag from the WebLogic Server instance you would like to debug.

Place these into your domain config repository (`config.xml`):

```
<Server Name="myserver" >
....
    <ServerDebug Name="myserver" JDBCConn="true" JDBCSQL="true"
JTAJDBC="true" />
</Server>
```

Alternatively, these debug flags can also be set as system properties during WebLogic Server start:

```
-DWebLogic.Debug=WebLogic.JDBCConn,WebLogic.JDBCSQL,WebLogic.JTAJDBC
```

These debug flags and tracing can be very verbose, so please consider very carefully where you turn on these flags. They will create a lot of output and also possibly have a performance impact on your system.

JVM hang pattern

When other components like JDBC or JMS can cause problems, the JVM can run out of memory. So if you're not sure, investigate the JVM. The causes mentioned next could be the root cause of the problem:

- **Binary Core File Analysis** – Using the tools as described before.

- **Irrecoverable StackOverFlow** – An application gets "an irrecoverable stack overflow has occurred. Unexpected Signal 11" message right before the JVM dies or core dumps.

- **Unexpected High CPU Usage with WLS** – A system administrator or user notices that the WebLogic Server process is consuming a lot of CPU cycles and wants to know why/what is consuming CPU cycles.

- **Too Many Open Files** – A system error "Too many open files" is reported in the WebLogic Server log. Users may see this as either `java.net.SocketException`: Too many open files OR `java.io.IOException`: Too many open files. Setting the `ulimit` to a proper value (in the `/etc/security/limits.conf`) could prevent these errors.

- **Missing Execute Threads** – The missing threads issue is discovered during analysis of a server hang problem or unexplained timeouts or other confusing and unexplained behavior. Look for threads that have died in the dump you have created (kill -3 `<process_number>`).

- **Out of Memory/Memory Leak Problems** – An application displays "Out of Memory" errors due to memory exhaustion, either in Java heap or native memory.

Debug your JVM Garbage Collect

To get more information about how the JVM is doing, you can add `-verbosegc` flag in the Java command line. The command differs from JDK vendor, as shown in the following table. After opening the `gc` log by adding `-verbose:gc`, it will print GC activity info to `stdout/stderr`. Or redirect to the `gc.log` file you have configured in the latter option. You can add them in your WebLogic startup script.

Oracle JRockit	SUN JDK
`-verbose:gc`	`-verbose:gc`
`-Xverboselog:gc.log`	`-Xloggc:gc.log`

JMS problems

When you suspect a JMS component, such as a queue or a topic or connection factory, is causing the problems, here are some hints which could help to identify a possible cause.

You could enable debugging for JMS, by adding:

```
-DWebLogic.debug.DebugJMSBackEnd=true
```

And in the startup options:

```
-DWebLogic.log.StdoutSeverity="Debug"
```

Or use the WebLogic Server Administration Console to set the debugging values.

Another action you could take is to enable JMS message logging

You can enable or disable JMS message logging for a queue, topic, JMS template, uniform distributed queue, and uniform distributed topic using the WebLogic Server Administration Console.

This can be done in the Administration Console; expand **Services | Messaging | JMS Modules**. In the **JMS Modules** table, click the JMS module that contains the configured resource. In the selected JMS module's **Summary of Resources** table, click the JMS resource that you want to edit.

WebLogic diagnostic tools

Oracle WebLogic Server delivers a variety of tools, which an administrator can use to monitor, debug, and analyze behavior of the many components that WebLogic consists of.

WebLogic Diagnostic Framework (WLDF)

This framework comprises a number of components that work together to collect, archive, and access diagnostic information. It gathers diagnostics real-time.

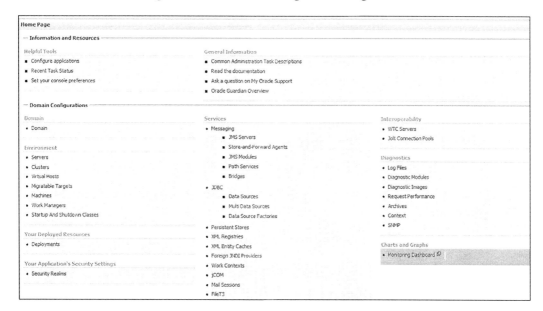

The following screenshot shows you the WLDF extension:

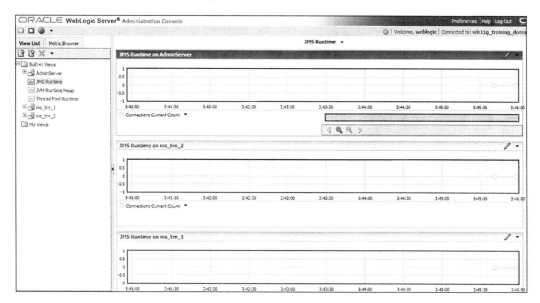

Application logging and WebLogic logging

Logging services provide information about server and application events, based on which you can analyze the possible problems. This will be handled in *Chapter 11, Configuring and Analyzing Logging.*

Some JVM consoles

Both shipped JDK's, JRockit and Sun's HotSpot deliver their own console to analyze the JVM behavior.

Oracle JRockit Mission Control

A nice console delivered with JRockit is the JRockit Mission Control.

It includes tools to monitor, manage, profile, and eliminate memory leaks in your Java application.

The following is a screenshot of JRockit Mission Control:

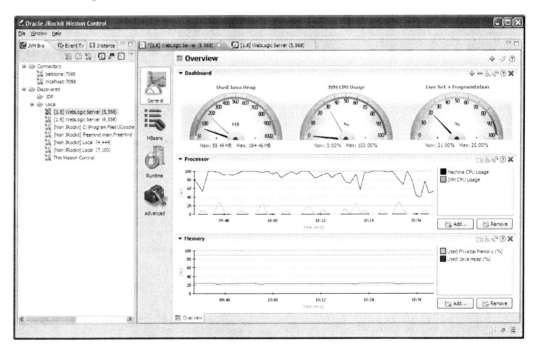

In here, you can create your connections to your WebLogic JVMs:

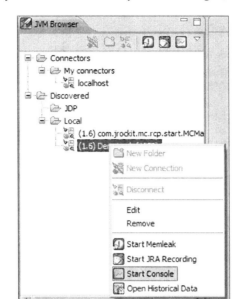

When connecting remotely, you should add the following start parameters for your JVM:

```
JAVA_OPTIONS="-Djava.rmi.server.hostname=<WebLogic Server> -Djavax.
management.builder.initial=weblogic.management.jmx.mbeanserver.
WLSMBeanServerBuilder  -Xmanagement:ssl=false,authenticate=false,autod
iscovery=true,port=7090"
export JAVA_OPTIONS
```

The port 7090 should be accessible from your own client.

Another useful option could be `-XX:FlightRecorderOptions=defaultrecording=true`, for having default recording when you connect.

There are several components to be found in JRMC such as:

- **JRockit Browser**: Browses several JRockit JVM instances and starts monitoring through the Management Console or the Memory Leak Detector.

- **Historical Data**: For trend watching; historical data is stored to get an overview over a longer period of time.

- **JRockit Runtime Analyzer**: To analyze recorded data with JRockit Flight Recorder.

- **Memory Leak Detector**: Detects memory leaks within your application.

- **Management Console**: To monitor live data from the JRockit JVM. This tool allows you to monitor the running Java application, create triggers that notify you when the condition is met and mail notifications.

There are two more things to get JRMC working with your WebLogic Server:

1. Do not forget to enable the Platform MBean and use of it in your WebLogic Admin Console. You can set it here on the Configuration Tab by clicking in the Domain in the left pane of the Admin Console.

2. Change the diagnostic volume of your WLDF to "High" in **Environment | Configuration | General**.

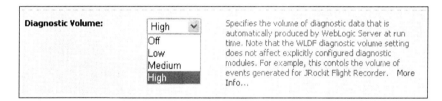

JConsole

JConsole is shipped as part of the Sun JDK, and doesn't require any specific download or installation.

In order to connect to a WebLogic MBeanServer, JConsole needs to be started as follows:

```
jconsole -J-Djava.class.path=$JAVA_HOME/lib/jconsole.jar:$JAVA_HOME/
lib/tools.jar:
$WL_HOME/server/lib/wljmxclient.jar -J-Djmx.remote.protocol.provider.
pkgs=weblogic.management.remote -debug
```

The previous code uses WebLogic's thin client classes. In some cases when you access server side classes, or you want to take full advantage of the t3 protocol, you are required to use WebLogic's thick client classes. To do so, you first need to build `wlfullclient.jar` as follows:

```
cd $WL_HOME/server/lib
java -jar wljarbuilder.jar
```

You can then start JConsole as follows:

```
jconsole -J-Djava.class.path=$JAVA_HOME/lib/jconsole.jar:$JAVA_HOME/
lib/tools.jar:
$WL_HOME/server/lib/wlfulclient.jar -J-Djmx.remote.protocol.provider.
pkgs=weblogic.management.remote -debug
```

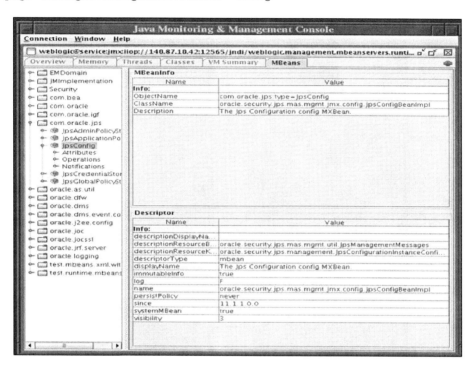

Additional: Oracle Enterprise Manager console

With a standard WebLogic Server installation, this component is not automatically installed. You will have to install ADF 11*g* runtime libraries and extend your domain with it.

When you have installed it, it's accessible through `http://<wl_hostname:ip>/em`.

The console has a rich set of tools such as performance overviews and extended diagnostic logging.

Basic WebLogic Server is not shipped with EM.

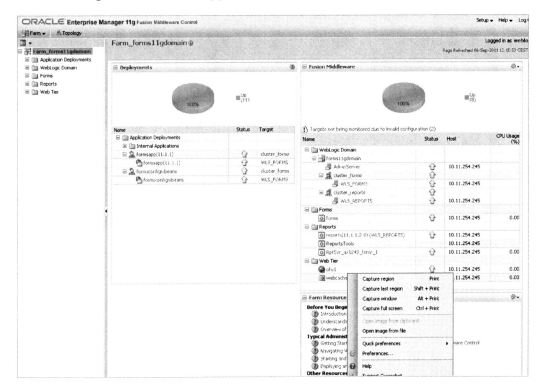

Summary

As you can see, Oracle WebLogic Server has a wide variety of options, possibilities, and tools in case something really goes wrong, but still it will be a tough job to discover the cause of an error and come up with a solution. This is also because of the complex IT infrastructure many companies have. A common best practice in the case of unclear problems is to form a team with all the right candidates, from a DBA to a network guy, and of course yourself, as the WebLogic administrator. That could help in detecting the cause of the problem and narrow down the options of systems in the chain that could fail.

An important topic that was left out of this chapter is Logging. This will be discussed in the next chapter.

11
Configuring and Analyzing Logging

Sailors sailing coast to coast across the seas always kept the records of their daily business in a book called a shipper's logbook. These contained all kinds of data, such as the ship's status, its location, the date and time, and a lot of other information about the ship and the crew.

In fact, computer systems maintain their status about many of these items too. These systems can give an overview, or unless configured in detail, about how your system was performing in the past and how it's performing right at this very moment.

So, let's take a deeper look into your Oracle WebLogic Server and also how to configure, maintain, and analyze your log files.

WebLogic Logging Services

WebLogic uses a mechanism called Logging Services to give detailed information about your WebLogic domain, server instances, resources, and applications.

Each WebLogic Server instance maintains a server log. Because each WebLogic Server domain can run concurrent multiple instances of WebLogic Server, the logging services collect messages that are generated on multiple server instances into a single domain-wide message log. The domain log provides the overall status of the domain.

Components of Logging Services

In fact, there are two main components that the logging mechanism depends on: the component that produces the logging and the other component that publishes the messages.

WebLogic uses the standard `java.util.logging` interface to let applications produce useful messages to the logging services. Applications can use two components:

- `weblogic.logging.NonCatalogLogger` APIs

  With NonCatalogLogger, instead of calling messages from a catalog, message text appears directly in your application code.

- Server Logging Bridge

  WebLogic Server provides a mechanism by which your logging application can have its messages redirected to WebLogic logging services without the need to make code changes or implement any of the proprietary WebLogic Logging APIs.

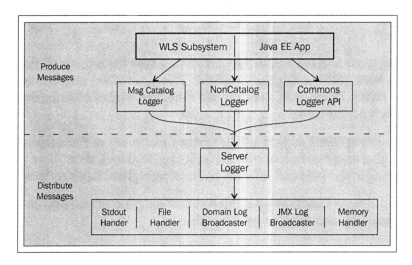

In the previous diagram, above the dotted line you can see the interfaces that produce Logging Messages. These produced messages are forwarded to the Server Logger interface, which—depending on the configuration of Logging—transfers the message through the several interfaces to a log file.

Oracle WebLogic Server logs

Oracle WebLogic Server logging services provide facilities for writing, viewing, filtering, and listening to log messages. These log messages are generated by the Oracle WebLogic Server instances, subsystems, and Java EE applications that run on Oracle WebLogic Server or on client JVMs.

Oracle WebLogic Server subsystems use logging services to provide information about events such as the deployment of new applications or the failure of one or more subsystems. A server instance uses them to communicate its status and respond to specific events. Debugging can also be enabled on individual subsystems to include additional life cycle information.

Some of the main subsystems that use logging services are:

- Server
- HTTP
- JTS
- JMS
- JDBC

Oracle WebLogic Server supports a variety of logging frameworks and is able to consume these log messages and redirect/publish them to a variety of destinations such as domain log files.

Logging Services—attributes/severities

When an Oracle WebLogic Server instance writes a message to the server log file, the first line of each message begins with #### followed by the message attributes. Each attribute is contained between angle brackets. The following is an example of a message in the server log file:

```
####<Sept 22, 2004 10:46:51 AM EST> <Notice> <WebLogicServer>
  <MyComputer> <examplesServer> <main> <<WLS Kernel>> <> <null>
  <1080575211904> <BEA-000360> <Server started in RUNNING mode>
```

The attributes each log file contains are as follows:

- **Timestamp**: The time and date when the message originated, in a format that is specific to the locale.
- **Subsystem**: The particular subsystem that was the source of the message (such as Management, Security, EJB, RMI, and JMS).
- **Severity**: The degree of impact or seriousness of the event reported by the message.
- **Catalog ID**: The unique ID assigned to this type of event, to reference in the online documentation.
- **Server Name**: The WebLogic Server instance that generated the message.
- **Machine Name**: The DNS name of the computer that hosts the WebLogic Server instance.

- **Thread ID**: The server thread that generated the message.

- **User ID**: The current security context, if any.

- **Transaction ID**: The current XA transaction context, if any.

- **Diagnostic Context ID**: Context information to correlate messages coming from a specific request or application.

- **Raw Time Value**: The timestamp in milliseconds.

- **Message ID**: A unique six-digit identifier.

- **Message Text**: A description of the event or condition.

Log severity level

Each log message has a severity level to determine the importance and urgency of a message. WebLogic Server delivers a severity level, from TRACE to EMERGENCY, which is converted to a log level when dispatching a log request to the logger. By default, servers forward only messages of the severity level NOTICE or higher.

The WebLogic Server subsystems generate many messages of lower severity and fewer messages of higher severity. For example, under normal circumstances, they generate many INFO messages and no EMERGENCY messages.

The following are the severity levels in WebLogic Server:

- **TRACE**: Messages from the diagnostics framework

- **DEBUG**: Detailed internal messages (if debugging is enabled)

- **INFO**: Normal operations

- **NOTICE**: INFO message of greater importance

- **WARNING**: Suspicious operation or configuration

- **ERROR**: Error-handling request, but no interruption in service

- **CRITICAL**: System or service error that may cause temporary loss or degradation of service

- **ALERT**: One or more services in an unusable state, requiring administrative attention

- **EMERGENCY**: Entire server in an unusable state

Server subsystem messages

The WebLogic Server catalog contains messages in the range from BEA002601 to BEA002799. Messages in this catalog are part of the `weblogic.Server` internationalization package and the `weblogic.i18n` localization package.

Server and domain logs

The WebLogic Server produces several types of log files. The first you encounter is called the server log. It logs all activity for a single server instance and is stored as `DOMAIN_HOME/servers/logs/SERVER_NAME.log` by default.

Another type of log file is the domain log. It logs key events from all servers in a domain and is stored in `DOMAIN_HOME/servers/SERVER_NAME/logs/DOMAIN_NAME.log` by default.

Other logs that WebLogic Server produces are:

- HTTP
- JMS
- JDBC

These logs are independently configured.

> Place the log files outside of the Domain Home; it is best practice to place them on a separate filesystem. In case of backup or recovery of a domain, the log files do not need to be recovered. Furthermore, to store log files on a central location can let you provide information to anyone who has an interest or goal to know how the WebLogic Server and its applications are doing.

Viewing log files

The following are some of the ways to view the content of a certain log file:

Viewing log files in the Admin Console

The easiest way to view logs is in the Admin Console by opening **Diagnostics** and selecting **Log Files** in the left pane of the console.

The page displays the latest contents of the log file—up to 500 messages in reverse chronological order. The messages at the top of the window are the most recent messages that the server has generated. Optionally, select the **Option** button next to any log message and click **View** to see its full details.

The log viewer does not display messages that have been rotated into the archive log files.

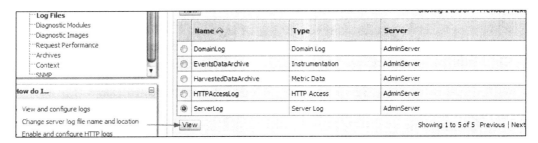

Using exportDiagnosticData with WLST

With WLST and the `exportDiagnosticData` command, you can view the contents of your log file without accessing the Admin Console. This can be done in WLST offline mode, although also at runtime, but there's no specific need to connect to the Administration Server.

The following is an example of how to do this:

```
wls:/offline> exportDiagnosticData (logicalName='ServerLog',
logName='myserver.log', exportFileName='myExport.xml')
Input parameters: {logicalName='ServerLog', logName='myserver.log',
logRotationDir='.', storeDir='../data/store/diagnostics', query='',
exportFileName='myExport.xml', elfFields='', beginTimestamp=0L, endTim
estamp=9223372036854775807L}
Exporting diagnostic data to myExport.xml ...
<Apr 3, 2009 11:23:56 AM EDT> <Info> <Store> <BEA-280050>
<Persistent store "WLS_DIAGNOSTICS" opened: directory="/u01/
app/oracle/product/fmw/11.1.0/wlserver_10.3/server/data/store/
diagnostics" writePolicy="Disabled" blockSize=512 directIO=false
driver="wlfileio2">
Exported diagnostic data successfully.
wls:/offline>
```

Viewing log files on the operating System

Another way of viewing log files is of course accessing the WebLogic Software owner on the physical host and viewing the log files with the tools available on the operating system. Linux has a wide variety of text manipulating tools such as VI or pico.

On the Linux command line, execute `tail -f <server-log>` can also be used on Linux for viewing logs in real-time.

The following screenshot shows the tailing a logfile:

Configure logging

WebLogic provides a standard way of how to deal with logging, but any administrator would adjust this to his/her needs. The following is an overview of how to configure logging in the most optimal way.

Configure logging using the Administration Console

When you want to configure logging, you can click on the name of a server instance whose logging you want to configure.

Click the **Logging | General** tab. The available options include:

- **Log file name**: The name of the file that stores the current log messages. If you specify a relative pathname, it is interpreted as relative to the server's root directory. The default is under the directory
  `<DOMAIN_HOME>/servers/<SERVER_NAME>/logs`

> Place the log files outside of the Domain Home; it is better to place them on a separate filesystem. In case of backup or recovery of a domain, the log files do not need to be recovered. Furthermore, to store log files at a central location can let you provide information to anyone who has an interest or goal to know how the WebLogic Server and its applications are doing.

- **Rotation type**:
  - ° **None**: Messages accumulate in a single file. You must erase the contents of the file when the size is too big. Note that Oracle WebLogic Server sets a threshold size limit of 500 MB before it forces a hard rotation to prevent excessive log file growth.
  - ° **By size**: When the log file reaches the size that you specified in **Rotation file size**, the server renames the file `FileName.n` with a number `3`.
  - ° **By time**: At each time interval that you specify in **Begin rotation time** and **Rotation interval**, the server renames the file with a number at the end.

Advantage of time: You have a log file for each day which could be useful for searching and storing later. You should only use this in development. Consider rotating the log file by size, rather than by time in production because with the time option in production, the file can grow large very quickly.

- **Limit number of retained files**: After the server reaches this limit, it deletes the oldest log file and creates a new log file with the latest suffix.

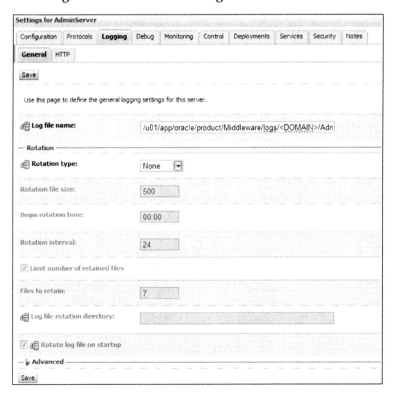

Configure Advanced Logging properties

When you want to configure some more options, you can click on the Advanced link. One of the sections is about **Logging implementation**. The Standard WebLogic Server uses the JDK implementation (`java.util.logging`). However, a developer sometimes uses another logging interface such as **Log4j**.

To change the default implementation, you can simply change it in the Administration Console under the Advanced Section of logging.

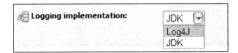

Integrating Application Logging

Application Developers can use the standard WebLogic Message catalog (the BEA-messages) for Application Logging. But when they want to have specific application logging, they will have to implement this by using the Java Logging APIs, Log4j, or the Commons API to produce and distribute messages.

Enabling Log4j Logging

To specify logging to a Log4j `Logger` instead of the default Java Logging:

- When you start the Administration Server, include the following Java option in the `weblogic.Server` command:

  ```
  -Dweblogic.log.Log4jLoggingEnabled=true
  ```

- After the Administration Server has started, use the Administration Console to specify the Log4j logging implementation.

- Use the WLST to set the value of the `Log4jLoggingEnabled` property and restart the server.

  ```
  wls:/mydomain/edit/Servers/myserver/Log/myserver !>
      cmo.setLog4jLoggingEnabled(true)
  ```

The developer should implement the Log4j classes into the code, and use a configuration file for using log handlers.

```
import org.apache.log4j.Logger;
import weblogic.logging.log4j.Log4jLoggingHelper;
import weblogic.logging.LoggerNotAvailableException;
```

The following is an example of a log handler:

```
<con:log>
    <con:name>myapp</con:name>
    <con:file-name>medrec.log</con:file-name>
    <con:rotation-type>bySize</con:rotation-type>
    <con:file-min-size>20000</con:file-min-size>
    <con:log4j-logging-enabled>false</con:log4j-logging-enabled>
</con:log>
<con:log>
    <con:name>myappServer</con:name>
    <con:rotation-type>bySize</con:rotation-type>
    <con:file-min-size>20000</con:file-min-size>
    <con:stdout-severity>Debug</con:stdout-severity>
    <con:stdout-filter>MyFilter</con:stdout-filter>
    <con:log4j-logging-enabled>true</con:log4j-logging-enabled>
</con:log>
<con:log-filter>
    <con:name>MyFilter</con:name>
    <con:subsystem-name>HTTP</con:subsystem-name>
    <con:subsystem-name>IIOP</con:subsystem-name>
    <con:subsystem-name>JDBC</con:subsystem-name>
    <con:subsystem-name>JMS</con:subsystem-name>
</con:log-filter>
```

Two other options to implement Log4j are to include the `wllog4.jar` file into the WebLogic Server's Classpath (in the `StartWebLogic` script) or to put the `wllog4.jar` file into the `<DOMAIN_HOME>/lib`.

The JarFiles `wllog4j.jar` is located in the `<WL_HOME/server/lib`.

Some other Advanced Logging settings

When clicking on the **Advanced** link you will find some other advanced options:

- **Logger severity properties**: Specifies the severity level for any specific logger.

- **Severity level**: Specifies the minimum severity of log messages that are to be written to the server log file.

- **Filter**: Specifies the filter configuration for the server log file. A filter configuration defines simple filtering rules to limit the volume of log messages written to the log file.

- **Redirect stdout logging enabled**: When enabled, redirects the standard out of the JVM in which an Oracle WebLogic Server instance runs to the WebLogic logging system.

- **Stdout severity Level**: Specifies the minimum severity of log messages going to standard out. Messages with a severity lower than the specified value are not published to standard out.

Stdout is an OS stream, which connects input and output channels between a computer program and its environment (typically a text terminal) when it begins execution. The three I/O connections are called standard input (stdin), standard output (stdout) , and standard error (stderr).

▽ Advanced	
Date Format Pattern:	MMM d, yyyy h:mm:ss a z
Minimum severity to log:	Info
Logger severity properties:	
Logging implementation:	JDK
☑ Redirect stdout logging enabled	
☑ Redirect stderr logging enabled	
☐ Logging Bridge Uses Parent Loggers	
Message destination(s)	
Log file :	
Severity level:	Trace
Filter:	None
Log File Buffer:	8
Standard out :	
Severity level:	Notice
Filter:	None
Domain log broadcaster :	
Severity level:	Notice
Filter:	None
Buffer Size:	1
Memory buffer :	
Memory Buffer Severity level:	Debug
Memory Buffer Filter:	None
Memory Buffer Size:	500
☑ Stack Traces to stdout	
stdout Stack Trace Depth:	5
stdout Format:	standard
Save	

Configure log filters

Why is it sometimes useful to implement filters in your logging?

With log filters you can control the log messages that are published. A filter leaves out messages of a certain severity level from a subsystem, such as JDBC or JMS, or according to a specified criteria (for example, only during peak hours). Only the log messages that satisfy the filter criteria are published. You can create separate filters for the messages that each server instance either writes to its server log file, stdout or memory buffer, or broadcasts to the domain-wide message log.

The default built-in filters such as severity levels filter out a lot already, but creating your own ones is really cool!

You can create a log filter by accessing the **Log Filters** tab in the Domain Home.

When you have created the log filter, you can add an expression you like to filter. We use a simple one: we only want to see the BEA-000360, Server Instance is "RUNNING".

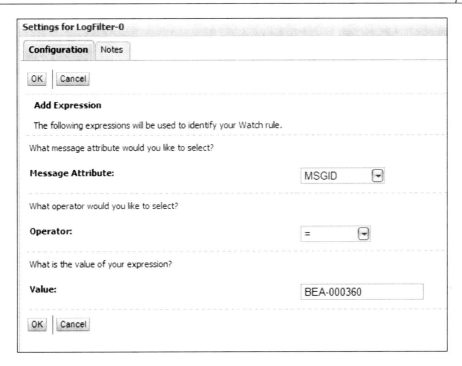

If you have saved your log filter, you will have to apply it. You must select the server instance on which you want to apply the filter. In the drop-down menu, your newly created filter should appear, as shown in the following screenshot:

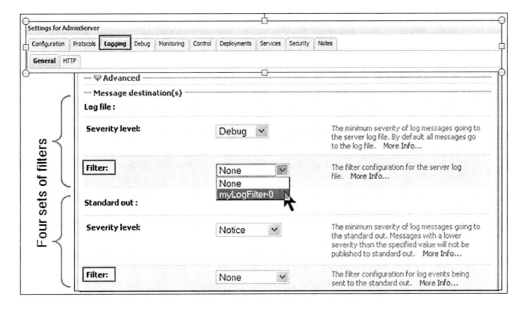

Oracle Diagnostics Logging (ODL)

Oracle Diagnostics Logging (ODL) (or better called Oracle Fusion Middleware Logging) is not shipped with the Oracle WebLogic Server software, but is part of an extension of additional installed Oracle Software such as the Oracle SOA Suite.

Although, as mentioned, it's not WebLogic logging, I'd like to mention it in a short overview because it's a very good extension on the already existing logging. Oracle Diagnostics Logging (or ODL) seeks to harmonize the different logging standards that have evolved among Oracle's products. The many differing standards make the management of several of Oracle's products a much more challenging task than is strictly necessary. As an administrator, you needed to learn and use several different methods. With ODL the log files can be managed in Enterprise Manager, centralizing the log file handling.

Log files and diagnostics can be shown within the Enterprise Manage Console. The developer can add the odl-handler into the code to make use of the ODL.

The administrator can, if Oracle Enterprise Manager is installed and added to the domain, view and search for ODL log files.

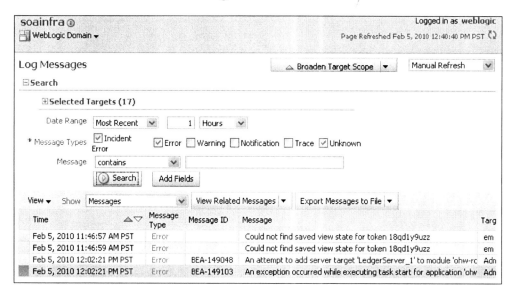

Summary

So, log files are pretty important in order to find out how your WebLogic Server, resources, and applications are doing, don't you think? If well configured, an administrator should find his/her way into determining the possible failures or bottlenecks, and come up with a solution.

Next, we will take a deeper look into who is authorized to have access to the Finance Fiction applications. Security is really a HOT issue nowadays!

12
Keeping your WebLogic Secure: Security and Protection

Finance Fiction. The company you work for is a global company with many customers working within the system built by your company.

One day, your boss came in with a group of security officers, and placed one at every door of each office, and locked each door with a key. "Everything needs to be secure!" he yelled in his usual stressed manner.

Later you heard your boss was assigned to maintain stricter security rules, but this—has he gone mad?

Well, maybe this is a bit over-exaggerated, but in a way your boss is quite right. Security begins at the front door of a company's building.

Security is a way to protect against damage, danger, and loss. In this chapter, we will talk about the security and protection of your Oracle WebLogic Server, but of course the issue of security extends much wider than securing and protecting your computer systems.

Of course your boss misunderstood his assignment, which in fact was all about maintaining security in the Finance Fiction computer environments.

Deploying, managing, and maintaining security is a challenge for your company that provides new and expanded services to customers using the Web. To serve a worldwide network of Web-based users, an organization must address the fundamental issues of maintaining the confidentiality, integrity, and availability of the system and its data. Challenges to security involve every component of the system.

Oracle WebLogic security concepts

Oracle WebLogic Server provides a security framework. It combines the security features of the WebLogic Server for application developers, system integrators, security administrators, and independent software vendors with a security platform. Developers can invoke the services provided directly from the development environment (Oracle JDeveloper) using wizards.

Administrators can configure the security services before and after the application is deployed into the Oracle WebLogic Server using Fusion Middleware Enterprise Manager, the Administration Console, or command-line utilities.

The Oracle WebLogic Security Service architecture

The WebLogic Security Service has the following components:

- A set of Security Service Provider Interfaces (SSPIs) for developing new security services that can be plugged into the Oracle WebLogic Server environment. SSPIs are available for Authentication, Authorization, Auditing, Role Mapping, Certificate Lookup and Validation, and Credential Mapping.

- A set of WebLogic security providers. These security providers are the Oracle implementation of the SSPIs and are available by default in the Oracle WebLogic Server. The WebLogic security providers include Authentication, Authorization, and Auditing. These providers can be used to authenticate against LDAP or Windows Active Directory.

- A set of Application Programming Interfaces (APIs) that allow application developers to specify authorization information that is used when Oracle WebLogic Server acts as a client and allow application developers to obtain information about the Subject and Principals used by Oracle WebLogic.

- J2SE security packages, including Java Secure Socket Extensions (JSSE), Java Authentication and Authorization Service (JAAS), Java Security Manager, Java Cryptography Architecture and Java Cryptography Extensions (JCE), and Java Authorization Contract for Containers (JACC).

This following diagram shows you an overview of Oracle WebLogic's security architecture:

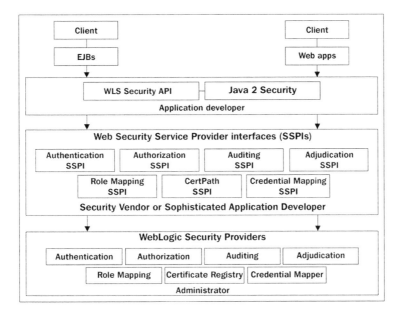

Oracle WebLogic security concepts

Authentication asks the question "Who are you?" using credentials such as username/password combinations to determine whether the caller is acting on behalf of specific users or system processes. In WebLogic Server, authentication providers prove the identity of users or system processes and transport and make identity information available to the components of a system (via subjects) when needed.

Authorization answers the question "What can you access?" based on user identity or other information. WebLogic Server provides an authorization provider to limit interaction between the users and the WebLogic resources to ensure integrity, confidentiality, and availability.

A simple authentication scenario

In this scenario, a user (or a client application), also referred to as the *subject*, attempts to log in to a system with a username/password combination. Oracle WebLogic establishes trust by validating that user's username and password. WebLogic Server passes the subject to the specified Principal Validation provider, which signs the principals and then returns them to the client application via WebLogic Server.

A *principal* is an identity assigned to a user or group as a result of authentication. The Java Authentication and Authorization Service (JAAS) requires that *subjects* be used as containers for authentication information, including principals. Whenever the principals stored within the subject are required for other security operations, the same Principal Validation provider will verify that the principals stored within the subject have not been modified since they were signed. When the user (subject) enters the user name and password, these properties and any other related information are encapsulated into the principal.

The validation of a principal is performed by the principal validator. After successfully proving the identity, an authentication context is established, which allows an identified user or system to be authorized.

During the authorization process, Oracle WebLogic determines whether it can perform a given operation on a given resource, and returns the result of that decision to the client application.

Roles are obtained from the Role Mapping providers and input to the Access Decisions. The Access Decisions are then consulted for an authorization result. If multiple Access Decisions are configured and return conflicting authorization results (such as PERMIT and DENY), an Adjudication provider is used to resolve the contradiction by returning a final decision.

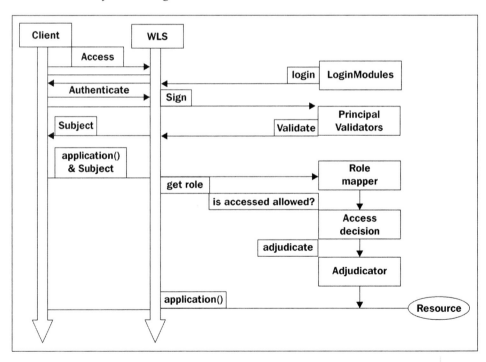

Security mechanisms used in WebLogic Server

WebLogic Server uses a mechanism to provide a secure environment, as follows:

Security realms

A security realm is a mechanism for protecting Oracle WebLogic Server resources, such as Authenticators, Adjudicators, Authorizers, Auditors, Role mappers, and Credential mappers. Resources in a domain are protected only under one security realm and by a single security policy in that security realm. A user must be defined in a security realm in order to access any resources belonging to that realm. When a user attempts to access a particular resource, WebLogic Server tries to authenticate the user and then authorize the user action by checking the access privileges that are assigned to the user in the relevant realm.

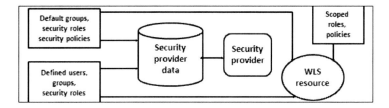

In the previous screenshot you can see the different components belonging to a security realm.

Users and groups

Users are entities that use WebLogic Server, such as:

- Application end users
- Client applications
- Other Oracle WebLogic Servers

A person can be defined as both an individual user and a group member. Individual-access permissions override any group member-access permissions. Oracle WebLogic Server evaluates each user by first looking for a group and testing whether the user is a member of the group and then looking for the user in the list of defined users.

Groups are:

- Logical sets of users
- More efficient for managing a large number of users

Groups can contain users or even other groups. This makes it easier to manage their security by giving permissions to a group instead of a single user.

By clicking on the **Security Realm** (myrealm is the WebLogic default) you can manage users and groups:

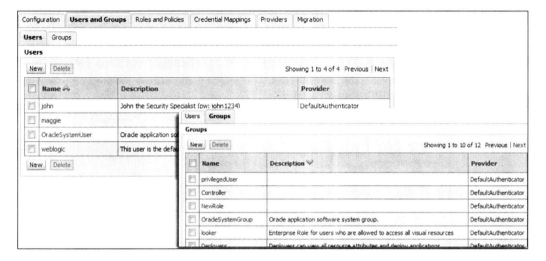

Users and Groups can both have one or many Group Memberships. WebLogic ships with a number of explicitly predefined groups like Administrators, Deployers, Operators, and Monitors.

WLS also has two implicitly predefined groups:

- *everyone* — authenticated and unauthenticated (something such as *public*)
- *users* — anyone who is authenticated or anyone with a known identity

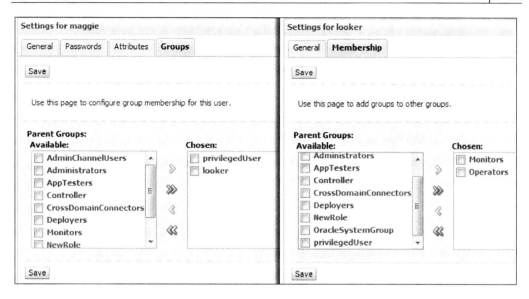

Roles and policies

A security role is a permission granted to users or groups based on several conditions. Just as for groups, security roles allow you to restrict access to WebLogic resources for several users simultaneously.

Security roles are assigned and granted to users or groups dynamically, based on conditions such as username, group membership, or the time of day, and can be scoped to specific WebLogic resources within an application in a WebLogic Server domain. Granting a security role to a user or a group confers the defined access privileges to that user or group as long as the user or group has the security role assigned. Multiple users or groups can be granted a single security role. A role definition is specific to a security realm.

WebLogic Server defines a set of default global roles for protecting all the WebLogic resources in a domain. A scoped role protects a specific resource, such as a method of an EJB or a branch of the JNDI tree. Most roles are scoped.

By default no security role is enforced and therefore all the resources can be accessed by any user.

Default global roles in WebLogic Server

- **Admin** can display and modify all resource attributes and perform start and stop operations. By default, users in the Administrators group are granted the Admin role.

- **Operator** can display all resource attributes. Users can start, suspend, resume, and stop resources. By default, users in the Operators group are granted the Operator role.

- **Monitor** can display all resource attributes. Users can modify the resource attributes and operations that are not restricted to the other roles. By default, users in the Monitors group are granted this role.

- **Deployer** can display all resource attributes. Users can deploy applications, EJBs, and other deployable modules. By default, users in the Deployers group are granted the Deployer role.

- **AppTester** can test the versions of applications that are deployed to the Admin mode.

- **Anonymous**: All users are granted this role.

These defaults are stored in an embedded LDAP directory, that is, the default to use for authentication.

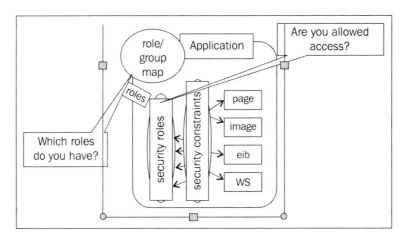

It is a full LDAP implementation, production quality, and suitable for up to 10k users. Even when an external LDAP is used for production, development and test could work with this embedded LDAP. The embedded LDAP is file-based—all data is stored in LDIF files stored in the domain.

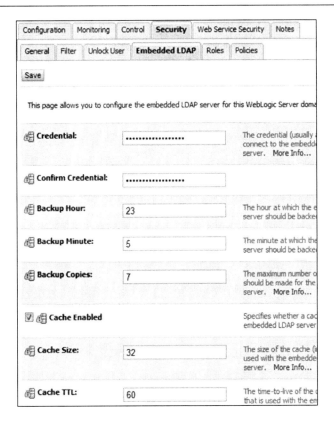

Application scope security roles

JEE already provides a standard model for securing Web applications and EJBs. In this standard model, you define role mappings and policies in the Web application or EJB deployment descriptors. But sometimes this JEE standard can be too inflexible for some environments, and in this case Oracle WebLogic Server has more flexible models to support the JEE standard.

Applications define security roles in their descriptor files:

- Web Application: `web.xml`
- Enterprise Java Bean application: `ejb-jar.xml`
- Enterprise Application: `application.xml`

```
<security-role>
    <description>
        HR is allowed to ...
    </description>
    <role-name>hr-department</role-name>
</security-role>
```

These can be inspected in the Admin Console; depending on application deployment, they may be editable.

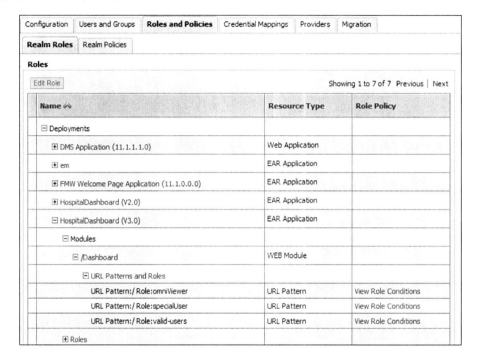

Security policies

WebLogic Server provides security policies and roles that are used together to control access to or protect resources. The security realm that WebLogic Server provides, stores policies in the embedded LDAP server.

You can create a root-level policy that applies to all instances of a specific resource type. Also, you can create a policy that applies to a specific resource instance. If the instance contains other resources, the included resource will inherit the policy as well. For example, you can create a policy for an entire EAR, an EJB JAR containing multiple EJBs, a particular EJB within that JAR, or a single method within that EJB.

Each policy has one or more conditions in it:

- **Basic**: This can be used to allow or deny access to everyone or specific users, groups, or roles.
- **Date and Time**: When you use any of the date and time conditions, the security policy grants access to all users for the date or time you specify.

- **Context Element**: You can use the context element conditions to create security policies based on the value of HTTP Servlet Request attributes, HTTP Session attributes, and EJB method parameters.

Authentication Providers

Authentication Providers are used to derive "Enterprise Identity" using login credentials, certificate or custom headers, using some form of LDAP, or other identity store. They can be configured in the Admin Console. There can be more than one active authentication provider.

The **Control Flag** governs whether authentication from a provider is required. If multiple providers are present, then at least one of them must be set to **REQUIRED**. You can mess up your domain resulting in not being able to start your server anymore (if you use two Authentication Providers, define the WebLogic user in both of them and set one to REQUIRED resulting in not being able to access the domain anymore). In fact, you should always set the DefaultAuthenticator to REQUIRED.

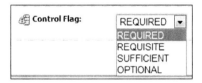

Providers can be created in the Security Realm under the **Providers** tab.

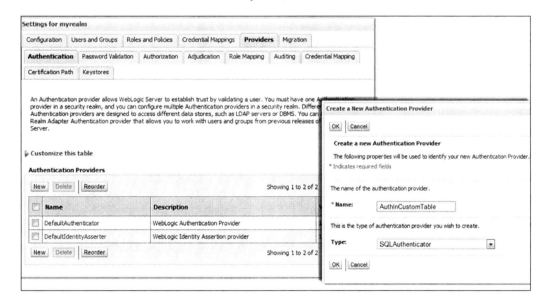

WebLogic Server also provides some third-party providers:

- LDAP Authentication providers for external LDAP
  - ° Stores Open LDAP, Microsoft Active Directory, Oracle Internet Directory, and Novell NDS

- DBMS authentication providers
  - ° Access security data in custom database schema

- Windows NT Authentication provider
- LDAP X509 Identity Assertion provider
- SAML Authentication/Identity Assertion
- Custom Authentication provider
  - ° For example, to work with third-party IDMs

The following screenshot shows the list of third-party providers:

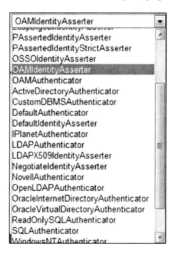

Credential mapping

A credential map is a mapping of credentials used by Oracle WebLogic Server for credentials that are used in a legacy (or a remote) system to connect to a given resource in that system. Credential maps allow your Oracle WebLogic Server to log in to a remote system on behalf of a subject that has already been authenticated.

A credential mapping provider of WLS can handle different types of credentials, such as username/password, and public key certificates. Credential mappings can be set in deployment descriptors of applications or through the Administration Console.

There can be multiple credential mapping providers configured in a security realm.

Other ways of protecting Oracle WebLogic

Securing Oracle WebLogic with authorization, authentication, and so on, is one thing, but there are some other ways to think of a solution to protect your resources.

Secure transport (for example, SSL)

SSL is the standard security technology for establishing an encrypted link between a Web server and a client.

Why use SSL Certificates:

- Verifying the legal, physical, and operational existence of the clients and/or servers.
- Verifying that the identity of the entity matches official records.
- Verifying that the entity has exclusive right to use the domain.

Single sign-on—share logon between apps

Using a central solution for user management such as LDAP can store user information for many applications and with this mechanism users can be assigned to the applications of their need. Because their password is stored in the LDAP, it's valid for all the applications to which they are assigned. They do not need to logon over and over again with every new application they use.

Prevention of/protection against attacks

These days, the term cyberwar is very real. All kinds of companies and their computer systems are being attacked by intruders using all kinds of techniques such as:

Man-in-the-middle attacks

In the "man-in-the-middle" attack, an unknown party (the attacker) poses as a destination host intercepting messages between the client and the real host. Instead of issuing the real destination host's SSL certificate, the attacker issues his/her own certificate hoping that the client will accept it as being from the real destination host.

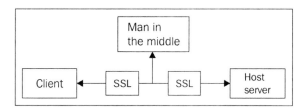

A Hostname Verifier is useful when an Oracle WebLogic Server or a WebLogic client acts as an SSL client to another application server. It prevents the "man-in-the-middle" attacks.

The **SSL** tab for the specified Server Instance is used to configure the **BEA Hostname Verifier**. It ensures that the hostname in the URL to which the client connects, matches the hostname in the digital certificate that the server sends back as part of the SSL connection.

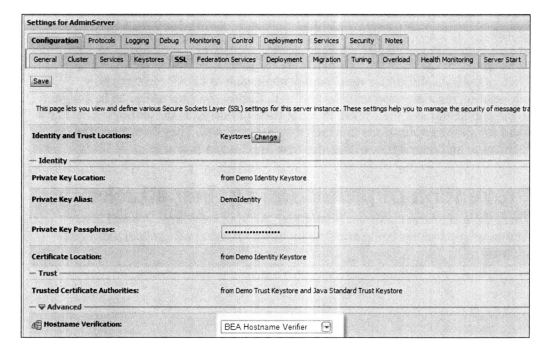

Denial of Service (DoS) attacks

Denial of Service (DoS) attacks can disable your computer or your network. Depending on the nature of your enterprise, this can effectively disable your organization.

Some DoS attacks can be executed with limited resources against a large, sophisticated site. This type of attack is sometimes called an "asymmetric attack". For example, an attacker with an old PC and a slow modem may be able to disable much faster and more sophisticated machines or networks.

A well-known method of attack is to bombard the target machine with external communication requests, such that it cannot respond to legitimate traffic. Attacks of this origin are called "floods". Others can be like disrupting specific services or systems.

Countermeasures against DoS attacks for WebLogic Server could be as filtering IP addresses using the `ConnectionFilter` interface. This can be done in the top-level domain from the Admin Console on the **Security | Filter** tab.

There is a default connection filter class called `weblogic.security.net.ConnectionFilterImpl`.

So no implementation is required if that fullfills your requirements. More information can be found at `http://download.oracle.com/docs/cd/E12839_01/apirefs.1111/e13952/taskhelp/security/ConfigureConnectionFiltering.html`.

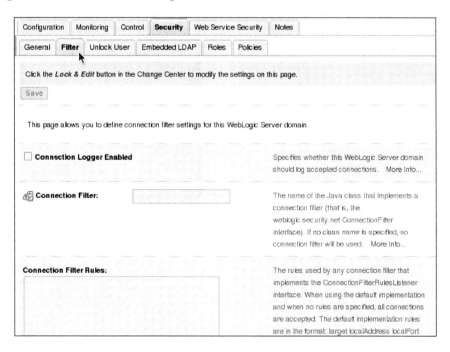

Large buffer attacks

A large buffer attack is an attack where a program, while writing data to a buffer, overruns the buffer's boundary and overwrites adjacent memory. This is a special case of violation of memory safety.

Hackers send large buffers of data to the server that starves the server of memory. WebLogic Server can be set to limit the amount of HTTP data that can be posted to its servers. This can be done using the Administration Console to manage this threshold. Any requests that exceed this threshold are denied access to the server. This can be done on a specific Server Instance tab, **Protocols | HTTP** tab in the right pane.

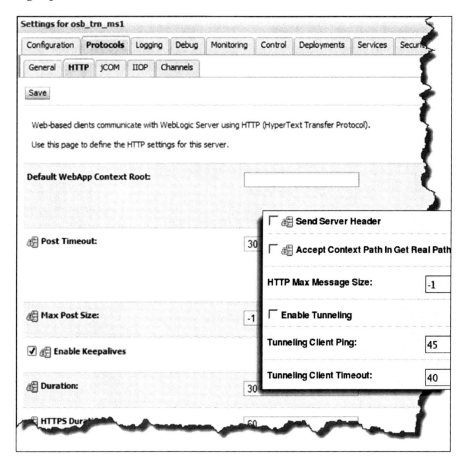

Connection starvation attacks

Sending small, incomplete messages to the server creates starvation attacks. The server then waits for the completion of the message, in effect unduly burdening the server. You can set a threshold for the time Oracle WebLogic Server will wait for the completion of the message.

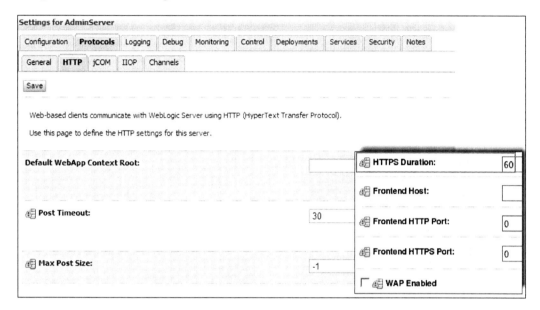

Summary

In this chapter, you have encountered the many aspects of being secure in your environment. As said, it begins with simple things, like not spreading usernames and passwords. Or providing everyone an access card.

The final chapter of this book should make your life much easier now. Let's talk about WebLogic Scripting Tool.

13
WLST: Makes an Administrator's Life Easier

For the past few months now, you have made yourself familiar with all the different aspects and concepts of your Oracle WebLogic Server environments. You have installed, configured, and deployed applications and used all your gained knowledge to have perfectly working environments.

One day, you were we're asked by the project team to work on a solution to script deployment tasks. Until now, the deployment was done using the Administration Console, but the team was looking for a better solution for automating this.

However, you are now trying to find a way to ease up administration work, and also be repetitive in the way you create WebLogic environments, do deployments, and so on.

One way to meet this requirement is embedded in Oracle WebLogic Server — the WebLogic Scripting Tool.

The WebLogic Scripting Tool explained

From Version 8x, a new and powerful tool was introduced, called WLST. WLST is a command-line tool that you can use to create, manage, and monitor WebLogic domains. WLST is a tool which is based on the Python programming language and uses the Jython feature to act as an administrator interface of the WebLogic Server. In addition to supporting standard Jython features — such as local variables, conditional variables, and flow control statements — WLST provides a set of scripting functions and commands that are specific to the WebLogic Server.

The Python language

WebLogic Scripting Tool, or let's call it WLST, is based on a programming language called Python. Python is an interpreted, interactive, object-oriented programming language. *Interpreted* means that the code is executed by a program that translates it into machine-code at runtime. It is *interactive* because it writes parts while it is already active. It uses modules, exceptions, dynamic typing, very high-level dynamic data types, and classes. It has interfaces to many system calls and libraries, as well as to various window systems, and is extensible in C or C++. It is also usable as an extension language for applications that need a programmable interface, in our case for Jython/WLST. Python is portable, that is it runs on many UNIX variants and all kinds of Windows versions.

Sometimes when using WLST, it's useful to use some pure Python functions to get information about operating system-specific information.

The Jython module

Jython is an implementation of the Python language in Java. It compiles Python code into Java bytecode and uses the JVM for this purpose. WLST uses Jython to access various objects within the WebLogic Server domain. These objects are called MBeans (Managed beans), that is Java objects that represent resources to be managed.

JMX

JMX or Java Management Extensions is the management interface to access the MBeans structure. MBeans must follow the design patterns and interfaces defined in the JMX specification. There are various ways to connect to the MBeans, for example a protocol connector such as the JMX RMI connector exposes the MBeans as they are, so a remote client sees the same model as a local client. Another way of connecting can be by using a protocol adaptor such as an SNMP adaptor or HTML adaptor. In fact, WLST is a JMX client that uses the HTML adaptor.

MBeans

An MBean is a simple Java object that is used to provide a management interface for an underlying resource.

- It is registered in the *WebLogic MBean Server* under a unique name under which it can be looked up and accessed
- It has named and typed attributes that can be read and/or written
- It has named and typed operations that can be invoked
- It has typed notifications that can be emitted by the MBean

The available MBean trees are:

- `domainConfig`
  - ° Configuration hierarchy of the entire domain; it represents the configuration MBeans in `RuntimeMBeanServer`
  - ° Is read only

- `serverConfig`
  - ° Configuration hierarchy (configuration MBeans) of the server you are connected to
  - ° Is read only

- `domainRuntime`
  - ° Hierarchy of runtime MBeans for the entire domain
  - ° Is read only

- `serverRuntime`
  - ° Hierarchy of runtime MBeans for the server you are connected to
  - ° Is read only

- `edit`
  - ° Writable domain configuration with pending changes; it represents the configuration MBeans in the `EditMBeanServer`

- `jndi`
  - ° Read-only JNDI tree for the server you are connected to

- `custom`
  - ° List of custom MBeans
  - ° Can be hierarchical/grouped if MBeans use namespaces appropriately

WLST wraps MBean access for popular operations, supports 'basic' JMX access for all MBeans, and allows direct interaction with MBeans.

The modes of WLST

WLST can be used in several modes:

- **Offline**: Analogous to the Configuration domain wizard
- **Online**: Analogous to the Administration Console

- **Interactive**: Command-line mode to prototype/verify scripts
- **Scripted**: Running Jython scripts sequentially without entering input
- **Embedded**: Use WLST interpreter from within your Java code

Offline mode

The offline mode can be used to create domains from a template shipped with WebLogic Server or by using your own created template. It's in fact the configuration wizard in command or scripted mode. In this mode, you need not connect to a running WebLogic Server, which sounds plausible. When you want to create a domain, there is no running server instance yet. During offline mode, one cannot view runtime performance or modify security data.

The offline mode is not recommended to do configuration changes because they can be overwritten by JMX clients, such as WLST online or the Administration Console. Also, you need to be running WLST locally for offline mode. You need filesystem access to the domain''s config folder.

The following script is a very simple example of an offline script to create a domain:

```
wl_home='/app/oracle/Middleware/wlserver_10.3'
# Open a domain template.
readTemplate (wl_home + '/common/templates/domains/wls.jar')
cd('Servers/AdminServer')
set('ListenPort', 7001 )
set('ListenAddress','10.0.0.12')
create('AdminServer','SSL')
cd('SSL/AdminServer')
set('Enabled', 'True')
set('ListenPort', 7002)
cd('/')
cd('Security/base_domain/User/WebLogic')
cmo.setName('WebLogic')
cmo.setPassword('webl0gic ')
setOption('OverwriteDomain', 'true')
setOption('ServerStartMode', 'prod')
writeDomain(domaintarget)
closeTemplate()
```

- Creating a domain (offline)
    - ° Create a new domain using a specified template:
      ```
      createDomain(domainTemplate, domainDir, user, password)
      ```
    - ° Open an existing domain template for domain creation:
      ```
      readTemplate(templateFileName)
      ```

- ° `writeDomain (domainDirName)`
- ° `closeTemplate ()`

- Updating an existing domain (offline)
    - ° Open an existing domain for update: `readDomain(domainDirName)`
    - ° Extend the current domain: `addTemplate(templateFileName)`
    - ° Save the domain: `updateDomain()`

Online mode

When connecting WLST to a running Administration Server, you can manage the configuration of an active WebLogic domain and view performance data about resources in the domain. You can also use WLST to connect to Managed Servers, but you cannot modify configuration data from Managed Servers; because this should only be done by the Administration Server since it is responsible for maintaining, updating, and storing the configuration data. During online mode, one cannot create a domain.

Example of an online mode:

WLST online: Connecting to a domain

- Setup the environment:
    - ° Set `WLSEnv.sh`(in `WL_HOME/server/bin`)
    - ° Add WebLogic server classes to `classpath` and `WL_HOME/server/bin` to `path`
- Invoke WLST:
    - ° `java weblogic.WLST`
- Starts in offline mode
- Connect to a domain:
    - ° `wls:/offline>`
      `connect('weblogic','weblogic','localhost:7001')`

Interactive mode

In the interactive mode, you can enter a command and view the response at the command-line prompt; it is useful for learning the tool, command syntax, and verifying configuration options before creating a script. When using WLST interactively, you will get immediate feedback after making a critical configuration change. The WLST shell keeps a connection with an instance of the WebLogic Server.

With the interactive mode you can browse through the complete MBean structure, navigating with certain commands.

WebLogic Server runtime MBeans are arranged in a hierarchical data structure. When connected to an Administration Server, you access the runtime MBean hierarchy by entering the `serverRuntime` or the `domainRuntime` command. The `serverRuntime` command places WLST at the root of the server runtime management object, `ServerRuntimeMBean`; the `domainRuntime` command places WLST at the root of the domain-wide runtime management objects called the `DomainRuntimeMBean`. When connected to a Managed Server, the root of the runtime MBeans is `ServerRuntimeMBean`. The domain runtime MBean hierarchy exists on the Administration Server only; you cannot use the `domainRuntime` command when connected to a Managed Server.

Using the `cd` command, you can navigate to any of the runtime child MBeans. The navigation model for runtime MBeans is the same as the navigation model for configuration MBeans. However, runtime MBeans exist only on the same server instance as their underlying managed resources (except for the domain-wide runtime MBeans on the Administration Server). Also, they are all uneditable.

Browsing with the WLST command-line needs a specific syntax such as:

- `ls(),ls('c'),ls('a')`
- `cd('/…')`

When you use the `easeSyntax()` command, all quotes and brackets can be left out. Beware, this is only when you don't have to change a configuration. So this is not recommended for scripted mode and especially when using loop constructs. You can also use the regular Jython syntax with parentheses after you enabled the easy syntax. To leave the easy syntax mode, just execute the `easeSyntax()` command again.

Scripted mode

When you become an expert in WLST, you'll be able to write your own scripts for administering your WebLogic Server and automate manual tasks. To run in scripted mode, you must invoke the script with the WLST command. This can be done in two ways:

- Directly on an OS command-line:
  ```
  java weblogic.WLST script.py
  ```

- Or execute the script in the WLST command-line:
  ```
  java weblogic.WLST
  Initializing WebLogic Scripting Tool (WLST) ...
  ...
  ```

```
...
wls:/(offline)> execfile('script.py')
starting the script ...
```

Because you always have to start with a connection to a domain , you should embed the connect-string to your WebLogic domain in the following way:

```
connect('<weblogic username>','<weblogic password>','<weblogic
    admin url>')
```

To use `weblogic.WLST`, you should run the `setWLSEnv` or the `setDomainEnv` script.

The `setWLSEnv` script is in the WebLogic Server Home, that is under the `wlserver_10.3/server/bin` directory.

The `setDomainEnv` script is in your Domain Home, that is in the `bin` directory. You can execute this by running the following code:

```
. ./setDomainEnv.sh
```

The same counts for the `setWLSEnv.sh` script.

Finally, WebLogic Server is shipped with some preconfigured shell-scripts, located in the `<WebLogic Server Home> /common/bin/wlst.sh`.

Embedded mode

To include WLST in Java programs, you can embed the code. This makes it possible to call the WLST interpreter from within your Java code.

For an administrator, the embedded mode is difficult to maintain, but the following is a small example:

```
package wlst;
import java.util.*;
import weblogic.management.scripting.utils.WLSTInterpreter;
import org.python.util.InteractiveInterpreter;
public class EmbeddedWLST
{
  static InteractiveInterpreter interpreter = null;
  EmbeddedWLST() {
    interpreter = new WLSTInterpreter();
  }
private static void connect() {
    StringBuffer buffer = new StringBuffer();
    buffer.append("connect('weblogic','weblogic')");
    interpreter.exec(buffer.toString());
  }
```

```
    private static void createServers() {
        StringBuffer buf = new StringBuffer();
        buf.append(startTransaction());
        buf.append("man1=create('msEmbedded1','Server')\n");
        buf.append("man2=create('msEmbedded2','Server')\n");
        buf.append("clus=create('clusterEmbedded','Cluster')\n");
        buf.append("man1.setListenPort(8001)\n");
        buf.append("man2.setListenPort(9001)\n");
        buf.append("man1.setCluster(clus)\n");
        buf.append("man2.setCluster(clus)\n");
        buf.append(endTransaction());
        buf.append("print 'Script ran successfully ...' \n");
        interpreter.exec(buf.toString());
    }
    private static String startTransaction() {
        StringBuffer buf = new StringBuffer();
        buf.append("edit()\n");
        buf.append("startEdit()\n");
        return buf.toString();
    }
    private static String endTransaction() {
        StringBuffer buf = new StringBuffer();
        buf.append("save()\n");
        buf.append("activate(block='true')\n");
        return buf.toString();
    }
    public static void main(String[] args) {
        new EmbeddedWLST();
        connect();
        createServers();
    }
}
```

Operational use of WLST

Of course, you want to use your WLST for operational purposes. As a beginner, you start with some simple commands, and the more knowledge you get, the more advanced is the way you use WLST.

Here are some examples how to use WLST for operational tasks:

Starting WebLogic Server instances

You can use WLST to start, stop, suspend, or manage the lifecycle of your Server instances. This can be accomplished in two ways:

Starting with the Node Manager

The following diagram explains that you can connect to the Node Manager using WLST, and from there you can stop or start your WebLogic Server instances:

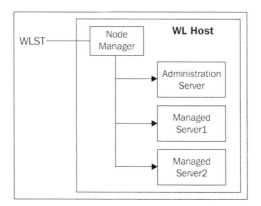

1. First, of course you will have to start up WLST, using:

   ```
   java weblogic.WLST
   ```

2. In the WLST console, notice the '**Offline**' in the prompt. Next type the following command to connect the Administration Server:

   ```
   connect('weblogic','Welkom123','t3://localhost:7001')
   ```

   When ready, notice the change in the prompt.

3. First, if it's necessary, start the Node Manager:

   ```
   startNodeManager(verbose='true',
   NodeManagerHome='<Node Manager Directory>', ListenPort='5556')
   ```

4. In the WLST shell, execute the following command to connect to the Node Manager:

   ```
   nmConnect('weblogic', '<weblogic password>','<weblogic
   host>','<nodemanager port>','<name of domain>,'<domain
   dir>','plain')
   ```

   The 'plain' stands for whether the connection is SSL or not. In this case, it's not.

 Type the command help('nmConnect') for detailed information on the void in the function nmConnect(void). If you get syntax errors, review the paths and names in the void; a typo is to be expected.

5. In the WLST shell, type the following command to view the status of the
    Managed Server `ms_trn_1`:

    ```
    nmServerStatus('<WebLogic Server Instance>')
    ```

6. If the status is *running* use the following command to stop the
    Managed Server:

    ```
    nmKill('<WebLogic Server Instance>')
    ```

    Verify that the server is *SHUTDOWN* using the `nmServerStatus` command.

7. Use the following command to restart the Managed Server `ms_trn_1` and
    review the feedback:

    ```
    nmStart('<WebLogic Server Instance>')
    ```

8. When the Node Manager is done, use the command `nmServerStatus` to
    review the current status.

Starting without the Node Manager

In this overview, you will connect via the Admin Server — instead of the Node
Manager — to manipulate the WebLogic Server instances. But this can even be
used in offline mode, and can be used to start up the Admin Server:

```
startServer('AdminServer', '<name of domain>','<Admin URL>',
'weblogic','<password WebLogic>', '>,'<domain dir>','true')
```

The following is a sample script that checks the status of a specific Server instance
and starts it when it is not running:

```
# Connect WLST to the running server
connect('weblogic','<password WebLogic>','<Admin URL>');

#The following command will print the state of the servers
print 'Status',state('AdminServer','Server');
serverRuntime()
a = get('State')
if a == 'RUNNING'
print 'Status',state('<Managed Server Name 1>','Server');
print 'Status',state('<Managed Server Name 2>','Server');

startServer('AdminServer','mydomain','<Admin URL>',
'weblogic','<password weblogic>', >,'<domain dir>','true')

# Disconnect the WLST from Adminserver
disconnect();
```

Using CMO (Current Management Object)

CMO is the WLST inbuilt variable. These are like our Java keywords having a dedicated meaning and functionality. CMO stands for Current Management Object. While using or programming in WLST, you can use `cmo` to point the current MBean (object) instance you are navigating to. The `cmo` value changes when you navigate to a different hierarchy of MBeans under different MBean trees in WebLogic (except for the JNDI tree).

When WLST first connects to an instance of WebLogic Server, `cmo` is initialized to the root of all configuration management objects which are of the `DomainMBean.MBean` type, the value of `cmo` reflects the parent MBean. MBean name gives the name of the MBean object.

```
wls:/mydomain/edit> cmo.setAdministrationPort(9005)
```

If you log in using WLST, `cmo` gives you the root MBean:

```
wls:/forms11g_domain/serverConfig> cmo
[MBeanServerInvocationHandler]com.bea:Name=forms11g_domain,Type=Domain
```

WLST deployment

WLST has a built-in deployment interface, from which you can deploy applications or update domain configurations. WLST deploys applications to a WebLogic Server instance similar to the `weblogic.Deployer` utility. The deploy command returns a `WLSTProgress` object that can be used to check the status.

In order to build a good deployment script, you should get to know the different editing commands you will have to use during deployment:

The following are the editing commands:

- `edit();`: Used to create, delete, get, set
- `startEdit();`: Starts new edit session
- `validate();`: Validates changes before saving
- `save();`: Saves your changes to a pending version
- `activate();`: Starts distribution of changes and releases session lock
- `stopEdit();`: Stops current editing session and releases session lock
- `isRestartRequired('true');`: Requires change, restart

Using WLST, you will have to use the various statements that contain the following commands in order to deploy an application:

- `deploy`: Deploy an application to a WebLogic Server instance
- `distributeApplication`: Copy the deployment bundle to the specified targets
- `getWLDM`: Return the WebLogic DeploymentManager object
- `loadApplication`: Load an application and deployment plan into memory
- `redeploy`: Redeploy a previously deployed application
- `startApplication`: Start an application, making it available to users
- `stopApplication`: Stop an application, making it unavailable to users
- `undeploy`: Undeploy an application from the specified servers
- `updateApplication`: Updates an application configuration with a new plan

The following is an example of a small deployment statement:

```
wls:/mydomain/serverConfig/Servers> deploy('App',
'<path of application package>', targets='<server instance>',
planPath='<path to deployment plan>', timeout=120000)
```

With the `progress.getState()` command, you can see the status of the deployment.

For more deployment techniques and know-hows, I'd like you to refer to *Chapter 6, Deploy Your Applications in Oracle WebLogic.*

Using WLST as an ANT task

It is possible to embed WLST commands into your ANT scripting, because Oracle WebLogic provides an ANT task for this, called `wlst`.

If you want to use the `wlst` task with your own ANT installation, include the following task definition in your build file:

```
<taskdef name="wlst"
    classname="weblogic.ant.taskdefs.management.WLSTTask" />
```

To use the ANT command, you will have to run the `setWLSEnv.sh` script from the WebLogic Server Home or the `setDomainEnv.sh` script from the Domain Home to run it from command-line and set all environment settings correctly.

When invoking WLST from an ANT script, it is recommended that you fork a new JVM by specifying `fork="true"`. This will ensure a clean environment and prevent the WLST `Exit` command—which calls `System.exit(0)`—from exiting the ANT script.

For deployment, you can use the `wldeploy` to add it to your ANT task. For this, you will have to include the following code into your build file:

```
<taskdef name="wldeploy" classname="weblogic.ant.taskdefs.management.
WLDeploy"/>
```

Then you can start using the `wldeploy` tasks as shown in the following example. It shows a `wldeploy` target that deploys an application to a single WebLogic Server instance:

```
<target name="deploy">
  <wldeploy
    action="deploy" verbose="true" debug="true"
    name="DeployExample" source="output/redeployEAR"
    user="weblogic" password="weblogic"
    adminurl="t3://localhost:7001" targets="myserver" />
</target>
```

Using the Console Script Recording feature

If you want to explore the capabilities of WLST and how to build scripts, you could use the Recording feature for the Admin Console:

First log into the Admin Console:

Step 1: Turn on recording

- Log in to the WLS console and click on '**Record**' (in the toolbar near the top of the page). This starts the WLST script recording. When you start recording, the console prints out the name of the WLST script file that it will create.

- Make some changes and turn off script recording. The recording session has started.

- Any configuration changes you make will be recorded in this script. Remember the name of this script since you'll be hand editing it later.

> Deployment plan changes and security data changes (such as adding, deleting, and modifying users, groups, roles, and policies) will not be captured in the script.

Step 2: Use the WLS console to make typical edits

- Use the WLS console to make some changes to the domain's configuration. For this example, create a new server in 'Cluster', enable SSL for the server, and customize the server's listen address, listen port, and SSL listen port.

Step 3: Turn off recording

- Click on '**Record**' again in the toolbar near the top of the page. This stops WLST script recording. The console will print out the name of the script again.

Messages

✓ The recording session has ended. Script recorded to /u01/app/oracle/product/Middleware/user_projects/domains/forms11g_domain/Script1310313818735.py.

You now have a script that shows how to add a new SSL-enabled server named 'MyServer' to the cluster 'MyCluster':

```
startEdit()
cd('/')
cmo.createServer('MyServer')
cd('/Servers/MyServer')
cmo.setListenAddress('MyListenAddress')
cmo.setListenPort(7777)
cmo.setCluster(getMBean('/Clusters/MyCluster'))
activate()
startEdit()
cmo.setListenPortEnabled(true)
cmo.setJavaCompiler('javac')
cmo.setClientCertProxyEnabled(false)
cmo.setMachine(None)
cd('/Servers/MyServer/SSL/MyServer')
cmo.setEnabled(true)
cmo.setListenPort(8888)
activate()
startEdit()
```

If you look at this script, you'll notice that it isn't ready to use yet because:

- ° It doesn't connect to the Admin Server at the beginning or disconnect at the end; this is because the console is already connected to the Admin Server.

- ° It doesn't start 'edit' to tell WLST to use the 'edit' MBean Server. The Admin Server has several different MBean Servers. The 'edit' MBean Server is the one that lets you view and manage the domain's configuration.

- ° There should be extra 'activate' and 'startEdit' commands. This is because 'Automatically Acquire Lock and Activate Changes' is enabled (this preference makes every console page use a separate configuration editing session).

- ° The server name, cluster name, listen address, listen port, and SSL listen port values are hardcoded.

Step 4: Edit the script

- Make a copy of the captured script, then edit the copy to address these issues.

- Use 'connect' at the beginning of the script to connect to the WebLogic domain. To connect, WLST needs to know the Admin Server URL as well as the Admin username and password. You have two choices on how to get this information.

  ○ Prompt for them or get the information from the command line, then pass them to the 'connect' command. Don"t pass any parameters to the 'connect' command. Instead, always run WLST from the domain directory on the Admin Server's machine. When you do this, WLST can automatically figure out the username, password, and URL.

- Call 'edit' to tell WLST to use the Admin Server's 'edit' JMX Server and use 'disconnect' at the end of the script.

- Remove the extra 'activate' and 'startEdit' commands.

- Parameterize the script, specify the server name, listen address, listen port, and SSL listen port. The following sample prompts for them.

> Since this example wants to show how to add new servers to an existing cluster, it leaves the cluster name hardcoded in the script 'MyCluster'. This is typical. Most scripts want to parameterize some values and hardcode others.

The following is the edited script:

```
connect()
edit()
myServerName = raw_input('Enter server name:')
myListenAddress = raw_input('Enter listen address:')
myListenPort = int(raw_input('Enter listen port:'))
mySSLListenPort = int(raw_input('Enter SSL listen port:'))
startEdit()
cd('/')
cmo.createServer(myServerName)
cd('/Servers/' + myServerName)
cmo.setListenAddress(myListenAddress)
cmo.setListenPort(myListenPort)
cmo.setCluster(getMBean('/Clusters/MyCluster'))
cmo.setListenPortEnabled(true)
cmo.setJavaCompiler('javac')
cmo.setClientCertProxyEnabled(false)
cmo.setMachine(None)
```

```
cd('/Servers/' + myServerName + '/SSL/' + myServerName)
cmo.setEnabled(true)
cmo.setListenPort(mySSLListenPort)
activate()
disconnect()
```

You now have a parameterized WLST script that your administrator can use to add new SSL-enabled servers to `MyCluster` as the load goes up.

Now you can run the script and the `raw_input` statement enables you to fill in your own parameters.

Command-line editing in a UNIX environment

Not a standard WebLogic feature, but one I'd like to discuss as a bonus for your hard work, is the command-line editing feature.

In a UNIX environment, WLST does not provide any command-line editing capabilities. However, you can use a third-party tool, such as JLine, to provide line editing in WLST.

JLine provides the following editing capabilities:

- Command history
- Line editing
- Custom key bindings

For more information about JLine refer to `http://jline.sourceforge.net/index.html`.

To use JLine with WLST, follow the steps mentioned next:

1. Download JLine from `http://jline.sourceforge.net/downloads.html`.

2. Unzip the file and put the `JLine jar` into a directory on your machine. Add the `JLine jar` to the `CLASSPATH`.

3. Run JLine as follows:

   ```
   java jline.ConsoleRunner weblogic.WLST
   ```

4. Alternatively, you can copy the `$WL_HOME/common/bin/wlst.sh` script and then add `jline.ConsoleRunner` before `weblogic.WLST`.

The default keys in JLine are:

- ° *UP ARROW* and *DOWN ARROW* to move within the command history
- ° *Ctrl* + *N* and *Ctrl* + *P* to move within the command history
- ° *LEFT ARROW* and *RIGHT ARROW* to move within a command
- ° *Ctrl* + *B* moves to the previous character
- ° *Ctrl* + *G* moves to the previous word
- ° *Ctrl* + *A* moves to the beginning of the line
- ° *Ctrl* + *F* moves to the next character
- ° *Ctrl* + *E* moves to the end of the line
- ° *Ctrl* + *U* deletes all characters before the cursor
- ° *Ctrl* + *W* deletes the word before the cursor

On UNIX systems, JLine will execute the `stty` command to initialize the terminal to allow unbuffered input, using the `jline.UnixTerminal` class.

Summary

The goal of this chapter was to give you a starting point, to get familiar with the strong capabilities of the WLST, customizing WLST and custom MBeans features.

WLST is used by many advanced WebLogic administrators to ease up their administrator tasks, but it also gives you a good knowledge of how your Oracle WebLogic domain is built up, and how you can configure it and do tasks in a structured and automated way, which will increase the capabilities of your systems.

From this point, I advise you to write smart scripts for doing deployments, managing and configuring and monitoring the state of your entire WebLogic domain. At some point, you could integrate your scripts with other tools you use in your company, perhaps an ANT-based deployment tool, a versioning tool, or a monitoring tool.

Happy scripting!!

Index

Q

queues, JMS
  about 154
  creating 152

R

ResultSet object 137
RESUMING state 105
roles and policies, Oracle WebLogic security
    241
RUNNING state 105

S

SAP 28
script-based node manager
  about 107
  configuring 107
scripted mode 256, 258, 259
security, Oracle WebLogic
  about 236
  Application Programming Interfaces (APIs)
      236
  application scope security roles 243
  architecture 236, 237
  authentication 237
  authentication providers 245, 246
  authorization 237
  concepts 237, 238
  connection starvation attacks 251
  credential map 246
  Denial of Service (DoS) attacks 249
  global roles WebLogic Server 242
  groups 240
  Java Authorization Contract for Containers
      (JACC) 236
  Java Cryptography Extensions (JCE) 236
  Java Secure Socket Extensions (JSSE) 236
  large buffer attacks 250
  man-in-the-middle attack 248
  policies 241, 244, 245
  prevention of/protection, against attacks
      247
  realms 239
  roles 241

Secure Transport (SSL) 247
Security Service Provider Interfaces (SSPIs)
    236
Single Sign-On 247
users 239
Security Service Provider Interfaces (SSPIs)
    236
server core dump pattern
  about 198
  WebLogic Server performance pack 198
ServerHang
  about 206
  deadly embrace 206
  out-of-threads deadlock 207
  thread states 206
server states 80
Service Oriented Architectures (SOA) 13
servlet. *See* **Java Servlet**
setDomainEnv script
  JVM, starting 189, 190
setDomainEnv.sh script 68
setWLSEnv script 67
SHUTDOWN state 105
SHUTTING DOWN state 105
silent mode. *See* **WLS 10.3.3, silent mode**
    installation
Simple Network Management Protocol
    (SNMP) 91
Single Sign-On 247
staging mode 117
STARTING state 105
startManagedWeblogic script
  JVM, starting 189
  used, for starting 101
startManagedWeblogic.sh script 68
startup commands, JVM 186, 187
startup script
  about 73, 74
  administration console 82
  administration console, components 83
  administration console, disabling 86
  administration console, enabling 86
  administration port, setting 87
  boot identity file creating, java weblogic.
      Server used 78
  boot identity, issues 77, 78

W

Thank you for buying
Oracle Weblogic Server 11*g*R1 PS2: Administration Essentials

About Packt Publishing

Packt, pronounced 'packed', published its first book "Mastering phpMyAdmin for Effective MySQL Management" in April 2004 and subsequently continued to specialize in publishing highly focused books on specific technologies and solutions.

Our books and publications share the experiences of your fellow IT professionals in adapting and customizing today's systems, applications, and frameworks. Our solution based books give you the knowledge and power to customize the software and technologies you're using to get the job done. Packt books are more specific and less general than the IT books you have seen in the past. Our unique business model allows us to bring you more focused information, giving you more of what you need to know, and less of what you don't.

Packt is a modern, yet unique publishing company, which focuses on producing quality, cutting-edge books for communities of developers, administrators, and newbies alike. For more information, please visit our website: www.packtpub.com.

About Packt Enterprise

In 2010, Packt launched two new brands, Packt Enterprise and Packt Open Source, in order to continue its focus on specialization. This book is part of the Packt Enterprise brand, home to books published on enterprise software – software created by major vendors, including (but not limited to) IBM, Microsoft and Oracle, often for use in other corporations. Its titles will offer information relevant to a range of users of this software, including administrators, developers, architects, and end users.

Writing for Packt

We welcome all inquiries from people who are interested in authoring. Book proposals should be sent to author@packtpub.com. If your book idea is still at an early stage and you would like to discuss it first before writing a formal book proposal, contact us; one of our commissioning editors will get in touch with you.

We're not just looking for published authors; if you have strong technical skills but no writing experience, our experienced editors can help you develop a writing career, or simply get some additional reward for your expertise.

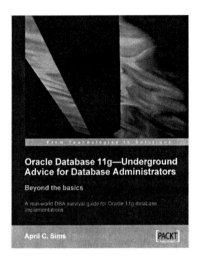

Oracle Database 11g – Underground Advice for Database Administrators

ISBN: 978-1-849680-00-4   Paperback: 588 pages

A real-world DBA survival guide for Oracle 11g database implementations with this Oracle book and eBook

1. A comprehensive handbook aimed at reducing the day-to-day struggle of Oracle 11g Database newcomers

2. Real-world reflections from an experienced DBA—what novice DBAs should really know

3. Implement Oracle's Maximum Availability Architecture with expert guidance

EJB 3.0 Database Persistence with Oracle Fusion Middleware 11g

ISBN: 978-1-849681-56-8   Paperback: 448 pages

A complete guide to building EJB 3.0 database persistent applications with Oracle Fusion Middleware 11g tools with this book and eBook

1. Integrate EJB 3.0 database persistence with Oracle Fusion Middleware tools: WebLogic Server, JDeveloper, and Enterprise Pack for Eclipse

2. Automatically create EJB 3.0 entity beans from database tables

3. Learn to wrap entity beans with session beans and create EJB 3.0 relationships

4. Apply JSF and ADF Faces user interfaces (UIs) to EJB 3.0 database persistence

Please check **www.PacktPub.com** for information on our titles

JDBC 4.0 and Oracle JDeveloper for J2EE Development

ISBN: 978-1-847194-30-5   Paperback: 444 pages

A J2EE developer's guide to using Oracle JDeveloper's integrated database features to build data-driven applications

1. Develop your Java applications using JDBC and Oracle JDeveloper

2. Explore the new features of JDBC 4.0

3. Use JDBC and the data tools in Oracle JDeveloper

Oracle 10g/11g Data and Database Management Utilities

ISBN: 978-1-847196-28-6   Paperback: 432 pages

Master twelve must-use utilities to optimize the efficiency, management, and performance of your daily database tasks

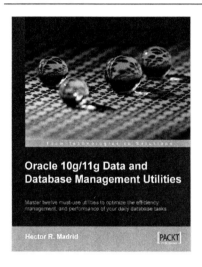

1. Optimize time-consuming tasks efficiently using the Oracle database utilities

2. Perform data loads on the fly and replace the functionality of the old export and import utilities using Data Pump or SQL*Loader

3. Boost database defenses with Oracle Wallet Manager and Security

4. A handbook with lots of practical content with real-life scenarios

Please check **www.PacktPub.com** for information on our titles

Lightning Source UK Ltd.
Milton Keynes UK
UKOW030335290911

179434UK00002B/135/P